Prepared Libraries, Empowered Teams

ALA Editions purchases fund advocacy, awareness, and accreditation programs
for library professionals worldwide.

Prepared Libraries, Empowered Teams

A Workbook for Navigating Intellectual Freedom Challenges Together

Becky Calzada,
Val Edwards, and
Maegan Coffin Heindel

Foreword by Steven D. Yates

CHICAGO | 2024

© 2024 by Becky Calzada, Val Edwards, and Maegan Coffin Heindel

Extensive effort has gone into ensuring the reliability of the information in this book; however, the publisher makes no warranty, express or implied, with respect to the material contained herein.

ISBN: 979-8-89255-537-1 (paper)

Cover design by Kimberly Hudgins. Composition by Alejandra Diaz in the Proforma and Fira Sans typefaces.

♾ This paper meets the requirements of ANSI/NISO Z39.48-1992 (Permanence of Paper).

Printed in the United States of America
28 27 26 25   5 4 3 2

*For the inspiring authors who write diverse books,
the voracious library users who check them out to read,
and the courageous librarians who defend and advocate
for access to those books in libraries.*
#FReadom
—B. C.

*For all our colleagues who strive every day to listen to the voices
in their communities and provide the content and access that they need and deserve.*
—V. E.

*For Silas, my heart:
so you always have windows, mirrors, and sliding doors in your reading life.*
—M. C. H.

CONTENTS

Foreword, by Steven D. Yates IX
Preface XI
Acknowledgments XIII
Introduction: Navigating Preparedness Planning XV

PART I — Words to Live By: Initializing the Challenge Readiness Plan

CHAPTER 1 Surveying the Current Landscape 3
CHAPTER 2 Identifying Existing Structures and Resources for Success 9
CHAPTER 3 Evaluating and Strengthening Your Policy Foundation 17

PART II — Words into Action: Operationalizing the Challenge Response Action Plan

CHAPTER 4 Readying Your Team for Cohesive Action 27
CHAPTER 5 Designing and Launching an Action Plan 33
CHAPTER 6 Establishing and Training for a Resolution Mindset 41

PART III — Words Take Flight: Systematizing the Challenge Readiness Plan

CHAPTER 7 Systems for Ongoing Readiness and Capacity-Building 57
CHAPTER 8 Planning for Clear Communication with All Stakeholders 63
CHAPTER 9 Applying Your Plan to Various Scenarios 71

Conclusion: Prepared and Empowered to Defend 77
Appendix: Team-Building Resources 79
About the Authors 81
Index 83

FOREWORD

Congratulations on one of the soundest decisions you have made this year! Picking up *Prepared Libraries, Empowered Teams: A Workbook for Navigating Intellectual Freedom Challenges Together* means that you have found a transformational tool in your community's conversation on intellectual freedom. Becky Calzada, Val Edwards, and Maegan Coffin Heindel have provided school and public library workers with an evergreen resource to guide work team empowerment far beyond our current cultural moment. This powerhouse trio of library leaders has graciously chosen to share their time, talents, and treasure trove of leadership and consulting experience with us in this highly accessible volume, and our profession is the better for it.

As Calzada, Edwards, and Coffin Heindel remind readers time and again, the path to being prepared always begins today. The moment you begin thinking about the health of intellectual freedom in your community is the moment to get started in parts I, II, or III of the following pages. Part I gives you the opportunity to understand what is currently happening in your community, what tools are currently available for you to use, and how those tools can be honed to provide the best support for intellectual freedom. While I agree with the talented trio that you need to start there, I see the true beauty and awesomeness of this text coming in parts II and III.

Parts II and III are the reminder that all readers need when thinking about intellectual freedom discussions. You cannot forget your own oxygen mask as you work to provide oxygen to your library team and their continued work for intellectual freedom in your community. The skills we all need to do intellectual freedom work to the best of our abilities take time, practice, and care. Calzada, Edwards, and Coffin Heindel generously guide readers through ways to respond to intellectual freedom challenges with equal doses of patience, poise, and preparedness—otherwise known as the three Ps—that we all need to maintain intellectual freedom in our communities. These three Ps are what make this workbook a unique contribution to your community's toolbox for intellectual freedom.

The three Ps are an incredible asset to any library worker as they work with patrons. The usefulness of this text goes far beyond intellectual freedom discussions. I especially appreciate the straightforward reminder that we prepare ourselves through practice to respond in any possibly tense moment with poise, especially when we remember to be patient with ourselves. *Prepared Libraries, Empowered Teams* weaves aspects of library and information science with public relations, conflict resolution, public speaking, and more. Countless school districts and library systems have paid consultants or developed their own team empowerment resources in house. That was before this incredibly useful tool was created.

As a former school and public librarian turned library educator, I am always looking for the best resources to help prepare my graduate students to be the resources their communities need for equity and access. This book is an immediate addition to my list of resources for both solo library workers and those who work in large systems and districts. Regardless of your work situation, this text provides a deliberate, thoughtful approach that will help you think about how to approach intellectual freedom questions (or any questions, really) in a measured way. But wait, there's more (said in my TV announcer voice)! It also reminds you repeatedly that any progress on the planning front is lost if you don't couple that planning with a commitment to onboarding all new team members, involve those outside of the library in your plans, and make practice a part of your team's schedule throughout each year. This work is not accomplished all at once, and this trio of professionals gives our profession just the guidance we need to make this work happen in the most productive and positive ways.

Thank you, Becky, Val, and Maegan. Our profession is better prepared for thoughtful action because of your work in the following pages and your recommendations for additional resources on team-building. Thank you also for the reminder that our teams extend far beyond any library walls, and so many folks stand ready to assist us as we support intellectual freedom in our communities. Let's get to work!

STEVEN D. YATES
Member, ALA Executive Board, 2023–2026
Chair, ALA Committee on Library Advocacy, 2021–2023
President, American Association of School Librarians, 2017–2018

PREFACE

Difficulties often bring people together. This is certainly true regarding the origins of this book. It began in 2022 when Val considered the recent increase in book challenges through a conflict resolution lens. Having worked as a consultant with many teams in conflict, she understood that team preparation would help libraries take a more unified, supported approach to managing challenges to intellectual freedom. She wanted to present on this timely topic at the American Library Association's (ALA) Annual Conference, and she wanted to collaborate with library leaders approaching this work in real time.

Fortunately for Val, Maegan had just received a position as a district library services coordinator. Val and Maegan had known each other for many years through their professional involvement in ALA and the American Association of School Librarians (AASL) and the Wisconsin AASL chapter called WEMTA. They were also library colleagues in the Madison, Wisconsin, area when Maegan was an elementary school librarian and Val was a high school librarian, as well as the district's lead librarian. Val reached out to Maegan about the possibility of presenting together, to which Maegan said yes immediately. Maegan also shared that she needed a library teacher-leader and thought Val would be a wonderful partner. Val said yes immediately. They began working together shortly after and immediately got started on assessing their district's challenge readiness.

Val also reached out to Becky Calzada, the library coordinator in Leander, Texas, to join in the session proposal as a co-presenter. Becky and Val had met in 2017 when Val worked for TeachingBooks.net and supported the setup and implementation of Texas's statewide license for those resources. Although their connection was limited, Becky was memorable in her dedication to providing high-quality resources for Leander students and supporting learning for the librarians on her team. These impressions have been strongly reinforced as Becky expanded her supportive efforts to colleagues around the country facing challenges, served as a cofounding member of the FReadom Fighters, and became president-elect of the AASL.

And so, the team was assembled, and the ALA session was submitted and accepted. Preparations for the presentation and our own district challenge preparations continued simultaneously. Becky was facing formal challenges, while Maegan and Val were navigating informal questions with their team, though not requests for reconsideration. When the time came to present, the response was overwhelmingly positive and the need for more resources on this topic was evident. We shifted our attention to expanding our ALA session into a book that could serve as an immediate resource for our library colleagues. We hope you find it useful on your journey, whatever your starting point.

ACKNOWLEDGMENTS

First and foremost, appreciation from the three of us to Jamie Santoro for the invitation, guidance, and encouragement to embark on this writing endeavor. Thank you, Jamie, the entire ALA Editions team, and Brittany Gitzlaff, for your insightful feedback on our many drafts.

My deep appreciation to the many professionals who coached me in my growth as a library leader, especially Carolyn Foote, Mary Woodard, Megan Cooper, and Dr. Carie Spannagel—your guidance played a pivotal role in my leadership journey. I am so very thankful for the Leander (TX) school district's librarians and library assistants—your hard work, dedication, and tireless energy inspire me every day. Catherine, Chandler, and Amanda—I love you all so very much! Your unwavering encouragement pushed me to seek out new opportunities—thanks for all you do behind the scenes to support me. My library journey would not be complete without a tip of the hat to my mom, Emma Hernandez, who was the person who took me to the public library in Mercedes, Texas—I never dreamed I'd be where I am today. You and dad believed reading and an education could change my life—you were right, and I love you both for your constant sacrifice for me and the family. Writing a book is no easy task, and I am thankful for my two coauthors, Maegan and Val, for your partnership in this endeavor and for inviting me to present with you at the 2023 ALA Annual Conference—who would have thought we'd end up here! —B. C.

To my colleagues within libraries and beyond who have become mentors, advisors, and lifelong friends, and to Dave, who has been willing to provide the space and resources for this career I love so much as it continues to evolve. —V. E.

I am forever grateful to the librarians who set me on my career path, and each gave me a different but essential lens on librarianship: Kim Dahl, Teresa Voss, and Jean Donham. I want to be them when I grow up! Many teaching partners, leaders, and students have provided learning experiences intentional and incidental throughout my teaching career. I appreciate my library team that put their trust in me to steer the ship, and that teach me more every day about being a leader and a librarian. Thank you to my coauthors for joining me in this endeavor; to Becky for generously sharing your depth of expertise, and to Val, whose invitation sparked a wonderful work partnership. To my husband Matt: thank you for keeping our household together so I could fulfill a dream. Thank you, Silas, for being excited for me to become an author. I love you both. Finally, thank you to my parents, who were always so proud of my writing skills and made sure I was surrounded by books of all kinds. —M. C. H.

INTRODUCTION
Navigating Preparedness Planning

This is a difficult time in the field. As library professionals are navigating increasingly intense intellectual freedom challenges, the fear of personal attacks and loss of employment is palpable; their determination to protect users' rights to books—books with complex and rich worldviews as well as books with diverse characters and cultures—is courageous in these unprecedented times. Their energies deserve to be sustained by deliberate actions taken by skillful and compassionate library leaders. We strive to be these leaders and hope to enable you to meet this need as well.

Over the course of our careers, we have managed questions and challenges about our library materials at different levels. At one end of the spectrum, we have fielded parental questions about the content of books in our collections, which were resolved through conversation and co-planning with families to help their readers select books to meet their reading needs and preferences. At the other end of the spectrum, our libraries have received inquiries from community members who demanded the immediate removal of books, sometimes bringing a list of multiple items. The latter have become more and more common, with a new level of intensity and publicity presenting new complications and calling for new approaches. At times, challenges like these can result in greater understanding and appreciation between professional and patron, but they can also surface anxieties and tensions between an organization and the community members it serves or within the organization itself.

Throughout every intellectual freedom challenge, our team's preparedness—or lack thereof—has been a key component in the relative success of both the resolution of challenges and the maintenance of team morale. We are continuously reflecting on and adjusting our organization's readiness to respond to challenges. Building a challenge-ready team is a never-ending process in which progress is achievable, but perfection is not. It is precisely because we are imperfect leaders that we feel compelled to share what we've learned in relatable ways that meet you where you are.

Whether a book challenge is upon you, on the horizon, in your rearview mirror, or not yet in sight, now is the time to start envisioning what a challenge-ready team would look like in your organization. The need for responsive plans, well-considered strategies, and coordinated teamwork is shared by all types of libraries. This book is intended for all library leaders in all kinds of libraries with teams of any size. Solo librarians too will find resources for coalition-building in the absence of library colleagues directly within their institution. By the end of this book, you will be equipped with tools and resources to tailor a challenge preparedness action plan to the needs of your library and community.

Expanding Your Viewpoint as You Plan

This book is organized in an inside-out manner. It starts from the foundational, inner-organizational workings that leaders must attend to before planning, and then we move to the action planning stage where the library team will be heavily involved. Finally, we widen the focus to include stakeholders within and outside the institution who need to know and live the plan (see figure 0.1 on the following page). However, because team-building is a major focus of this work, you will find recommendations for gathering team input and building team capacity throughout. You do not have to take your team through this process in a linear fashion. The unique needs and structures of your organization may dictate the order in which you tackle the tasks in this book. We have organized the book in an order that is logical to us in hindsight, but in reality, we each moved around the steps of challenge readiness in response to team needs as they arose.

Introduction

FIGURE 0.1

Challenge readiness concepts and audiences from the inside out

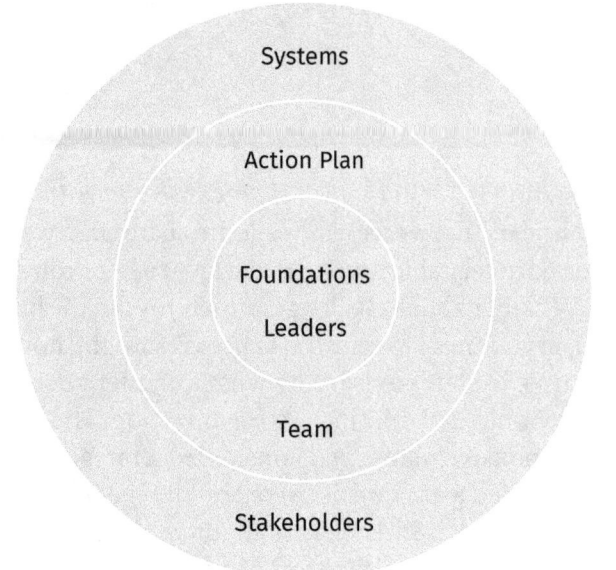

Your Challenge Readiness Road Map

Part I lays the foundation for your team approach by guiding a review of current circumstances and structures. We begin in chapter 1 with a survey of the national landscape. Then in chapter 2 we zoom in on your community climate, organizational status, and team members' strengths. In chapter 3, we provide considerations for developing strong policies and procedures on which your action plan rests. These policies and procedures, embodied in words on paper, create a living document to guide all that follows.

In part II, you will encounter practical suggestions for training your team for both the technical and relational aspects of action planning, and transforming the words of your policy and procedures into a functional blueprint for challenge readiness. Chapter 4 helps identify methods for developing deep knowledge of your organization's selection policy in your team members. At the same time, we address how to approach conflict and concerns within your team. Chapter 5 contains planning templates, strategies, checklists, and suggested scripts to assist in co-constructing a unified approach with your team. Chapter 6 focuses on preparing your team to implement the plan you create through professional learning and practice so that each member of your organization knows their role should a challenge arise.

Part III takes the action plan throughout your organization and beyond, providing best practices for communication and capacity-building in the

---

A FEW DEFINITIONS

When we talk about "teams" throughout this book, we refer to the group of people who operate your library or libraries and would potentially receive an intellectual freedom question from a library user. In public libraries, this is likely your entire staff, from library page to director. In a school district, the library team consists of school librarians, library assistants, and any library leaders and support people at the district office. We make it clear when it would be beneficial to focus on a smaller section of your team for expanded responsibilities specific to responding to a challenge.

We often use the word "challenges" as shorthand throughout the text, by which we mean intellectual freedom challenges. For our purposes, the term "challenges" encompasses both informal questions and formal requests for reconsideration from any source, particularly before they become official book bans. When we are referring to a specific type of challenge, we will call that out.

We use the term "inquirer" to refer to anyone who has raised a question or challenge regarding library materials. Sometimes the words "questioner," "complainant," or "challenger" are also used. We intentionally selected the word "inquirer" to represent that the question could be either formal or informal. More importantly, the term "inquirer" highlights that in essence an intellectual freedom challenge is a question, and so that word respects our library users' right to engage in dialogue with us about our library collections.

Finally, the terms "user" or "patron" are intentionally used when speaking generally about those whom we serve in all types of libraries. You can read these terms through the lens of your library type. A library user could be a child, teen, adult, learner, family member, college student, or any reader. A challenge could come from any of these individuals, and it is for them that we work to protect intellectual freedom.

face of all manner of challenges. Chapter 7 helps you systematize and maintain your action plan, while chapter 8 helps you be clear and intentional as you decide which stakeholders need what information and when. Finally, in chapter 9, you will find examples of various kinds of book challenges and how our approach to team preparedness might be applied.

In the conclusion, we reassert the strength of a cohesive team approach and reaffirm your power to influence and bolster your team through book challenges and, in turn, preserve the precious right to read.

Tools are embedded throughout the book, along with templates accessible via QR code, allowing them to be absorbed in conjunction with their related concepts. Several of these tools are also available at **alaeditions.org/webextras**. In this book, you will also find reflective prompts and note-taking space to capture insights and ideas for implementation and activation as they are generated. In the appendix, you will find recommended resource lists and potential partner and resource organizations.

As you read this book, we hope you absorb and embrace an overarching message: you do not have to go it alone.

PART I
WORDS TO LIVE BY
Initializing the Challenge Readiness Plan

Part I begins by taking stock of the elements that underpin your team's approach to challenges: politics, partnerships, policies, and procedures. Effective leaders do not enter a planning conversation unprepared, nor do they bring initiatives to their teams fully formed. They present an informed foundational structure and engage the team when the time is right. Walking this line requires knowing your team, institution, and community with all their potential and limitations. Start by examining the full scope of your current circumstances, from the culture in your organization and community to the reality of recent threats to intellectual freedom in our country. From this work, you will construct the basis on which your action plan rests.

CHAPTER 1

Surveying the Current Landscape

Libraries should challenge censorship in the fulfillment of their responsibility to provide information and enlightenment.
—ALA LIBRARY BILL OF RIGHTS

In recent years, there has been an onslaught of book challenges and bans across the United States. It is probable that you or someone you know has been directly impacted by a book challenge. ALA's Office for Intellectual Freedom (OIF) recorded 1,269 attempts to censor books and other resources in the United States in 2022. This was almost double the number of challenges it reported in 2021. The challenges in 2023 involved 4,240 different books and other materials. Schools saw 58 percent of these challenges, whether in school libraries or classrooms, while public libraries received 41 percent of the overall challenges in 2022. In just the first eight months of 2023, 3,923 total titles were challenged in 695 attempts (see figure 1.1 on the following page).[1]

While challenges to intellectual freedom are not new, challenges to multiple books at once are a much more recent development. In the first three quarters of 2023, 92 percent of all bans were part of an effort to ban multiple titles at once via a published list, whereas prior to 2022, most challenges had addressed just a single book at a time.[2] The scale, pace, and intensity of recent bans are unprecedented and unsettling. It has become common for politically motivated groups to encourage community members to bring a list of multiple suggested titles deemed "inappropriate" or even "pornographic" to their school and public library boards for reconsideration.[3] In addition, governing boards and administrators are pulling books from their own libraries' shelves. In one district, school board members pulled 125 books onto carts for review, immediately restricting access for students.[4] In some states, new legislation is prompting librarians to place restrictions on access or not purchase titles at all over fears that they will lose state library funding, face prosecution and fines, have their teaching licenses revoked, or lose their jobs.[5] Many librarians are leaving the field preemptively as the dialogue in their communities has turned ugly, with some people accusing librarians of having nefarious motives, doxing them, or even issuing threats of bodily harm. Though a national ALA poll in 2022 found that 70 percent of parents opposed book banning and largely trust their school and public librarians to make selection decisions, in many libraries a vocal few are limiting access to materials for the rest of their communities.[6]

Library users suffer when access to books is restricted. Students, families, and patrons of all ages have come to expect their library shelves to represent a wide swath of experiences and viewpoints. When books are removed from the shelves, or never make it there due to self-censorship in the selection process, library users miss out on materials that could reflect their own experiences or expand

FIGURE 1.1

Book ban data from ALA's Office for Intellectual Freedom

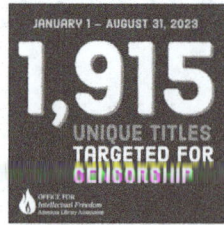

Source: Office for Intellectual Freedom, "Book Ban Data," American Library Association, March 20, 2023, www.ala.org/advocacy/bbooks/book-ban-data.

their worldview and develop empathy. Unfortunately, the books most frequently challenged represent our country's most historically marginalized groups. After studying a selection of books banned in schools in 2022, PEN America found that 30 percent of the titles included characters of color or dealt with topics of race or racism, and 26 percent of the titles featured LGBTQ+ characters or topics. They also discovered an emerging trend: book challengers have begun targeting materials that offer information on subjects related to health and well-being like grief, abuse, puberty, and teen pregnancy.[7] Access to reliable information on such impactful topics can be a lifeline for library patrons and must be protected.

Our Calling

If you are like us, recent statistics bring up a variety of emotions. Perhaps you feel anger, fear, helplessness, or a call to action. Our emotions run high because our passion for libraries and their mission is strong. No matter the type of library, librarians share similar values and an orientation for service, striving to meet the needs of all users. To this end, and despite barriers, librarians courageously seek to uphold the tenets of intellectual freedom, as indicated in ALA's Library Bill of Rights,[8] which maintains that "materials should not be excluded because of the origin, background, or views of those contributing to their creation" or "removed because of partisan or doctrinal disapproval." When selecting materials for collections, "the interest, information, and enlightenment of all people of the community the library serves" is top of mind for the library professional. Libraries uplift the voices of authors of color, whose works are just beginning to see a significant increase in publication, according to recent diversity statistics published by the Cooperative Children's Book Center (CCBC) at the University of Wisconsin–Madison (see figure 1.2).[9] Access to books and other information is essential to maintaining an educated populace in our democratic society. Literacy

FIGURE 1.2

2022 CCBC diversity statistics, by (Author/Illustrator/Compiler)

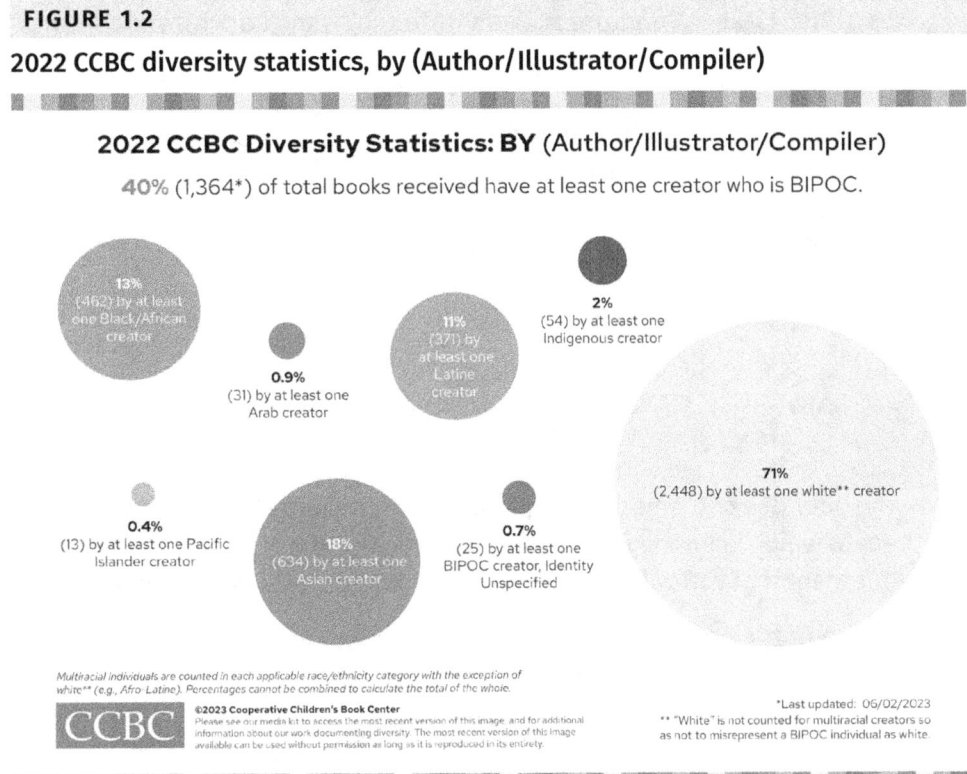

Source: CCBC, CCBC Media Kit, https://ccbc.education.wisc.edu/literature-resources/ccbc-diversity-statistics/.

and reading are a critical route to personal and societal improvement. Librarians take pride in providing and protecting free and equitable access to all kinds of materials for all kinds of users. Ultimately, we strive to accept and affirm the intersectional identities of our diverse library users—and the inhabitants of our nation—by representing them and their neighbors in the books we select.

Our Response

Considering the current challenges to representation, we believe library teams have a responsibility to protect the diversity of their collections in the face of growing restrictions. However, knowing how to navigate a book challenge requires intentional planning as well as emotional and structural support for librarians in the field. In the media, the most common story involves a single librarian facing scathing commentary and threats to their livelihood. The conversation has focused less on teams handling book challenges as a cohesive unit. Our approach centers on opportunities for preparing yourself and your team to merge into a single resilient entity, organized for the same purpose and pulling in the same direction. When multiple professionals with varied strengths, perspectives, and backgrounds co-create a set of guidelines and talking points, that team can launch a coordinated response to an attack on intellectual freedom.

By engaging in pre-planning for book challenges, you are able to:
- Prepare your library team for crises and develop a capacity to engage in difficult conversations around intellectual freedom.

- Establish clearer communication within the team and with the community.
- Develop policies and action plans for addressing a challenge and identify opportunities for improvement.
- Maintain the team's unity and integrity under stress.
- Support your team and prioritize their well-being.
- Seek additional partnerships so as to avoid isolation and strengthen your position.

CHRONICLE YOUR JOURNEY!

Share the intended outcomes of pre-planning for challenges with your full team. Ask them to weigh in on the following questions. Use that conversation to reassure your team that you will work together to develop challenge preparedness.

- Which of the benefits of pre-planning are most important to them?
- Where do they see current strengths and areas of need in your organization?
- What are their biggest concerns related to intellectual freedom?

_____

_____

_____

List your team or organization's shared values. How might you build on these to develop your team approach to book challenges?

_____

_____

_____

What is the ideal outcome for your team as a result of this work? What will it look like, feel like, and sound like if the team approaches a book challenge in a cohesive way?

_____

_____

_____

After reading this chapter, what ideas, questions, or action steps do you want to use to inform your work as you delve into challenge readiness preparations with your team?

_____

_____

_____

NOTES

1. American Library Association, "2023 Book Ban Data: Banned and Challenged Books," March 20, 2023, www.ala.org/advocacy/bbooks/book-ban-data.
2. American Library Association, "2023 Book Ban Data."
3. Madeleine Carlisle, "Public Libraries Face Threats to Funding and Collections as Book Bans Surge," *Time*, September 7, 2022, https://time.com/6211350/public-libraries-book-bans/.
4. Richard Hall, "'They Were Trying to Erase Us': Inside a Texas Town's Chilling Effort to Ban LGBT+ Books," *The Independent*, April 26, 2023, www.independent.co.uk/news/world/americas/texas-book-bans-granbury-lgbt-b2324468.html.
5. Ailsa Chang, "The Battle over Book Bans Takes a Toll on Librarians and Comes at a Financial Cost," August 11, 2023, in *Consider This from NPR*, podcast, audio, 16:06, www.npr.org/transcripts/1193446007.
6. American Library Association, "Large Majorities of Voters Oppose Book Bans and Have Confidence in Libraries," news release, March 2022, www.ala.org/news/press-releases/2022/03/large-majorities-voters-oppose-book-bans-and-have-confidence-libraries.
7. Kasey Meehan and Jonathan Friedman, "Update on Book Bans in the 2022–2023 School Year Shows Expanded Censorship of Themes Centered on Race, History, Sexual Orientation and Gender," PEN America, April 2023, https://pen.org/report/banned-in-the-usa-state-laws-supercharge-book-suppression-in-schools/.
8. American Library Association, "Library Bill of Rights," www.ala.org/advocacy/intfreedom/librarybill.
9. Claire Kirch, "Diversity Is on the Rise in Children's Literature," *Publishers Weekly*, June 13, 2023, www.publishersweekly.com/pw/by-topic/childrens/childrens-industry-news/article/92543-ccbc-releases-statistics-regarding-diversity-in-children-s-literature-published-in-2022.html.

CHAPTER 2

Identifying Existing Structures and Resources for Success

Alone we can do so little; together we can do so much.
—HELEN KELLER

When faced with a stressful incident like a book challenge, panic and fear can understandably spur one to act quickly. However, it is to you and your team's benefit when you slow down to survey your circumstances before formulating a plan. Understanding the current state of your workplace and community allows you to create a game plan that suits the unique qualities of both, as well as identify much-needed allies who will support you when facing book challenges.

If you are reading this and haven't yet experienced a challenge, you and your institution are in the fortunate position of being able to formulate that plan proactively. If you have already faced book challenges, it is not too late to reflect on and adjust your plan for efficiency, clarity, and cohesion.

Workplace Culture and Climate

First, take an honest look at your organization's strengths and needs regarding culture and climate. Consider the following questions:
- Does your team work well together or are there known areas of tension?
- Do you currently have systems in place for reaching consensus on decisions?
- Have these processes been contentious in the past?
- Are decisions largely made by those at the top, or are there opportunities for all to have their voices heard?

If you have strong systems for including all voices in conversations, you will need to activate those systems throughout the planning process. Consider from the beginning where and when you will include voices of the whole team versus when leadership will make the final call. Be transparent and inform your team as to which decisions are ultimately out of your hands. For example, your policies will need to be reviewed and adopted by your board, and even your departmental procedures likely need approval by a superior, depending on your organization's structure. Know when to take a step back and listen to team voices. If your organization has a history of conflict and difficulty in making team decisions, you need to openly address the ways in which past practices have not been working in order to move forward.

Collaborative Priority-Setting: A Strategy for Including All Team Voices

Adopting structured meeting protocols can ensure that all participants are heard and can make decision-making criteria more visible. These protocols also provide a moment to pause, reflect, and engage in more expansive thinking than our day-to-day routine usually allows. This is especially helpful for teams that are building toward more positive ways of working together. The following is one example of a strategy for gathering team input to guide decisions. For team members who might not feel comfortable speaking up in a whole-group setting, the pre-thinking and small-group sharing aspect of the following protocol can increase feelings of safety so their opinions can be heard.

Collaborative Priority-Setting

Purpose: Co-create a set of guiding priorities for teamwork incorporating all team members' input.

Materials Needed: Sentence strips, sticky notes, pens or pencils, markers, or a collaborative digital whiteboard space (i.e., Padlet, Figjam, Google Slides, etc.).

Procedures

1. Pose a question to the team and share the rationale for this protocol. For example, you might say: "At each challenge planning meeting, we will review the priorities we develop here to ground us and ensure we attend to our initial vision. Though these might evolve over time, returning to them helps us maintain our focus." Keep the prompt and a simplified list of the protocol steps visible throughout the process via a poster or projected slide. Take a variation on a question from the end of chapter 1 as an example, "What do you see as the biggest benefits of pre-planning for challenges for our library team?"
2. The team members think independently and record their ideas on sticky notes or in a designated space within a digital tool (i.e., an assigned slide). Set a timer for your desired amount of time so team members know what to expect. Leave enough time for them to expand beyond their first thought, but not enough that participants are waiting and off-task. We like 3–5 minutes, depending on the topic at hand.
3. In groups of 2–6, depending on the size of your team, ask participants to share their notes with each other. Foreshadow that they will be looking for themes and commonalities.
4. Ask each group to write 3–5 statements on sentence strips that encompass all their ideas. This work might take 7–10 minutes.
5. Group all the strips together to seek further commonalities between them. Attempt to craft 3–5 statements that encompass all the ideas suggested. During this time, attend to which voices are not being heard and consider calling on individuals who have not yet spoken.
6. Post the statements for consideration as team priorities. Solicit any final questions or recommendations that team members may have regarding the listed priorities. Ask participants to hold up one, two, three, or four fingers to indicate their support of the priorities. Four represents full agreement, while a one means the participant has major issues with the list.

Community Culture and Climate

Since book challenges most often come from the local community, it is essential that you understand its members' values and desires. As a patron-centered institution, your library likely already knows a lot about your users' interests and priorities. Now is the time to expand on that understanding by considering the perspectives of community members who do not frequent your library, as well as those of your local government officials.

To begin, identify the existing values of your workplace, both stated and implied. Your governing board and administration will want to hear how your challenge response plan fits in with their vision and goals. With your team, identify values that are in alignment with the tenets of intellectual freedom. For example, one of the stated values in the Madison (WI) school district is "belonging." Maintaining a diverse collection that represents all patrons is directly in support of the value of belonging.

When you know your community deeply, you can tailor your communication to ensure that it speaks to members' values. Your library visitors want to understand how you select books to represent a variety of viewpoints. Families need to hear that librarians want their children and teens to thrive, just like they do. Building positive relationships before conflict occurs not only gives you information about your community, but also puts valuable social capital in the bank that you can draw on during difficult interactions later.

Beyond Your Community

While each local community has its own unique set of circumstances, do not focus so locally that you ignore national and worldwide trends in intellectual freedom challenges. Be alert to new issues as they arise in the censorship landscape and ask your team members to do the same. Doing so strengthens your team's ability to anticipate new kinds of challenges, learn new ways to approach readiness, and identify new allies who are facing similar hardships.

Current Policies and Procedures

Board policies and organizational guidelines regarding selection and reconsideration are another area for review. Look with the intent to ascertain what structures and restrictions are currently in place and assess whether changes to the policies and guidelines are needed. Your board maintains a selection policy outlining who selects materials and the criteria for selection, plus a reconsideration policy that defines how a request for reconsideration can be submitted, who should be included in a reconsideration committee, and details about appeals. These policies have been adopted by your board and may be out of date. In most policies, the details are sparse and high-level, pointing to a second document, one that is often called "procedures" or "guidelines." Procedures and guidelines do not necessarily have to be approved by your library or school board and include much greater detail regarding the selection criteria and reconsideration processes.

Look at your policies and procedures regularly, beginning early in the process of challenge readiness planning. These rules vary greatly between organizations and can either protect your librarians and collections or leave them vulnerable. There are no right or wrong choices regarding these rules, as community and organization needs differ. However, below are some questions to ask when deciding whether your policies and procedures need attention. You will find a fully downloadable and editable checklist in the next chapter, which delves more deeply into policy-building.

- If you have an established policy on the books, when was the last time it was updated? Anything over two years warrants review.
- Does your policy include details on selection, deselection, and reconsideration? Do these rules connect to each other in logical ways?
- Does your current process of selection, deselection, and reconsideration match the wording in the policy? For example, we discovered that our policy's language on selecting material for weeding was no longer practical or sustainable and was not the actual practice we engaged in.

Opportunities at All Levels

Institutional Priorities

In addition to your department's policies and procedures, take time to consider how your book challenge processes fit into the larger operations of your institution. Your team's response to inquiries will not take place in a vacuum. It is essential that you look outside the silo of your library, department, or branch. Start at the levels closest to you and zoom out to the wider organizational parameters to consider.

What are your administrator's or supervisor's thoughts and feelings on this work? Think about the primary focus and priority for their workload. Because supervisors juggle multiple and varied tasks each day, it is important to present clear links between this endeavor and their work. Share how building solid team guidelines for challenges can help your supervisor lead with confidence during moments of stress. Tap into their connectedness within your organization and their knowledge of its politics to gain insight throughout your planning process and reduce friction as you move forward.

Read your organization's strategic plan and goals carefully. Where do their desired outcomes overlap with your library's mission? This background work prepares you to highlight shared priorities as you communicate with your leaders. They will appreciate your efforts to develop and maintain institutional cohesion and clarity.

Statewide Parameters

Does your state have legislation in place related to book selection, content, or the use of school/library funds? Your plan needs to operate within the confines of these laws. While this may seem obvious, it is important to consider these

---

Cracking the Code: Understanding the Climate of Your Community

Want to find out more about the current climate and disposition of your community? Here are some first steps:

- Read your local and regional papers, including smaller publications that may have different perspectives. Ask your teammates to bring you news items of note as well.
- Attend city council and school/public library board meetings. If you can't attend, you can usually find recordings or minutes posted online after the fact.
- Connect with your team members who are part of local organizations and boards to ascertain what conversations are taking place in the community.
- Utilize existing survey data, like school climate surveys, library patron surveys, or city-wide surveys conducted by outside organizations.
- Be present and visible in your community, regularly speaking to parents, patrons, students, and community members.

restrictions at the beginning of the process rather than try to retrofit a completed plan after the fact.

National Models

How well do you and your team know the professional tenets of intellectual freedom? Consider how you can marry the particulars of your department, organization, and state with ALA's guidelines. This work is not one-size-fits-all. Each library and community have a particular set of strengths, challenges, and norms to which you must attend while keeping broader ideals in mind.

Supporting Resources and Partnerships

It is important to take account of the relationships and connections you can draw on through the planning process and beyond.

Internal Allies

What other departments or branches within your organization would support your efforts or brainstorm with you? For school libraries, your district's Curriculum and Instruction Department is a natural partner, as they may also receive challenges to their curricular materials and have a different lens that can help you avoid a myopic approach. In public and other libraries, you should include Friends groups, Foundation leaders, or members of regional library systems in conversation from the beginning. In bigger systems, don't try to develop a process for your branch alone, but instead pull together with other branches for unity, consistency, and diversity of perspectives.

Interlibrary Connections

School libraries: reach out to your public library counterparts. Public libraries: talk to the school librarians. Both organizations are serving the same users and community and are likely facing the same issues, making this collaboration a natural fit. What conversations about intellectual freedom are taking place in university libraries in your area? If you haven't built relationships with these professionals, there's no time like the present.

Like-Minded Local Organizations

The Madison school district, for example, is incredibly fortunate to have access to the CCBC and their intellectual freedom resources that are available to Wisconsin libraries. Look for similarly focused groups in your community. Does your state employ individuals who are dedicated to overseeing libraries? Wisconsin's

Department of Public Instruction has a state school library consultant, as well as a public library consultant and digital learning colleagues. If such positions exist in your state, these professionals are excellent partners.

State and National Partners

What work is your state library association already doing in the area of intellectual freedom, including your ALA/AASL affiliates? What other reading-focused organizations exist in your state? State and national reading associations share your goal of championing literacy and thus are potential allies. National organizations, such as PEN America, exist to support the right to read. Because censorship touches all corners of the library world, many ALA divisions are addressing challenge readiness through webinars and resources. And of course, ALA's Office for Intellectual Freedom is a crucial partner. Have their contact information at hand.

Your Team as a Resource

Keep team cohesion and connection at the front of your mind during this stage of planning. Your current workplace culture informs the ways in which you will communicate with the team about both the planning stages and the actual response to a book challenge. You should think about the specific strengths and backgrounds that individuals or subgroups bring to the organization. This is your human capital, or the value your team members bring to your organization via their experience, knowledge, and skills (see figure 2.1). For example, the Madison school district maintains a Library Leadership Team made up of representatives

FIGURE 2.1

Human capital in the library team

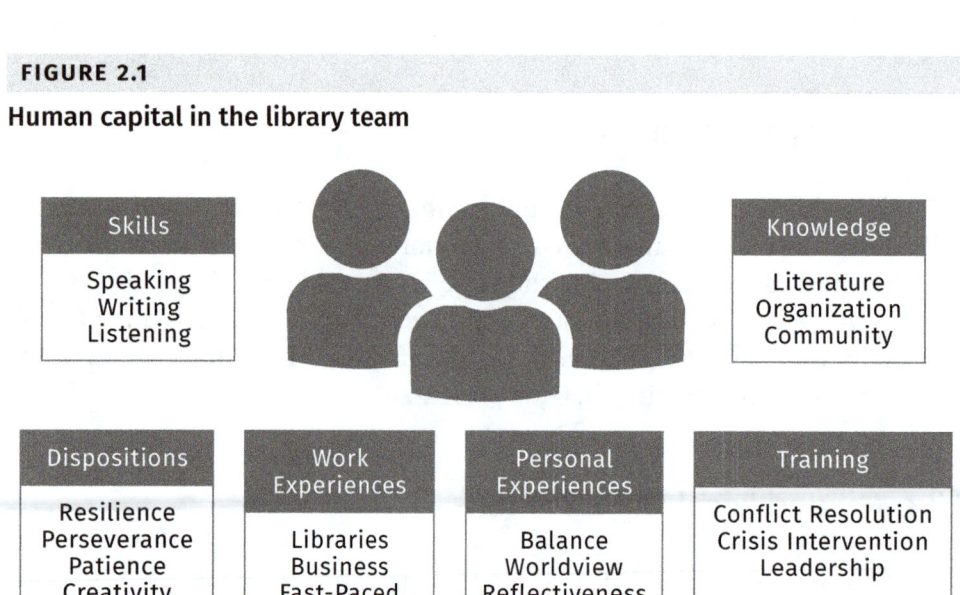

Team Triumph: The Power of a Unified Approach

A sixth-grader's parent contacted her middle schooler's school librarian to question the content of a book. Her learner had brought home a novel that contained strong language, and this parent preferred that her preteen's access to such language be limited. The school librarian wisely reached out to her district support team for input and assistance, which advised that she take some time before responding and request a meeting in person to discuss the parent's concerns. This allowed the librarian to calm her own nerves and prepare a plan. She would research book lists to assist the sixth-grader find books that would not contain strong language. The parent was relieved that the librarian affirmed her right to guide her learner's reading selections. The librarian was satisfied that she could retain book choices that would be suitable for other students.

While this situation was fairly uncomplicated to resolve, we quickly realized that there was no formally stated expectation that librarians would reach out for district support when receiving such inquiries. In addition, the librarian would have benefited from having a policy, scripts, and recommendations at her fingertips. Since we never know when a question will come up, we must always have resources at the ready. Reflecting on our past experiences helps us identify areas in need of development.

from elementary, middle, and high school libraries who apply to serve their colleagues as liaisons to district leadership for a two-year stint. This group structure is instrumental as we develop a strong team response to intellectual freedom challenges. Selected for their leadership qualities, the members of the leadership team are the go-to team for providing input, identifying priorities, and gathering questions or concerns from the broader team. Similarly, in the Leander (TX) school district, small ad hoc teams that can provide input on particular topics are selected based on their interests and strengths.

Thinking about the personalities and roles of your team members now prepares you for developing your plan and identifying the roles for each team member. Look for professional dispositions, skills, and knowledge that make individuals well-suited to particular types of work. Who is good at speaking calmly under pressure? Who has excellent research skills? Who can always recommend the perfect children's or young adult book? Which team members are naturally nurturing and supportive of their colleagues? Paying attention to your team's human capital will benefit you throughout your planning process and beyond.

As you consider your coworkers, adopt an assets-based lens. While no one is perfect, it benefits your process and relationships to focus on your teammates' strengths and how you can build on them, rather than on their limitations. Your team is the first line of communication to library users and thus the one most likely to be impacted by material inquiries. Be intentional about regarding your teammates with respect as valued partners.

CHRONICLE YOUR JOURNEY!

Which current team structures can you leverage as you begin this process? For example, what existing, effective communication systems or successful professional development schedules can be utilized to move this work forward? Which ways of working might hinder progress and need some further development?

_____

_____

_____

List your team or organization's shared values. How might you build on these to develop your team approach to book challenges?

_____

_____

_____

PART I | Words to Live By

What is the current landscape in your community? What are common conversations within and outside your organization regarding challenges to library materials? Have you already had requests for reconsideration? If so, what type of content was targeted?

_____

_____

_____

After reading this chapter, what ideas, questions, or action steps do you want to adopt as you delve into these conversations with your team?

_____

_____

_____

CHAPTER 3

Evaluating and Strengthening Your Policy Foundation

When a challenge arises, your policy will be the north star: laying out the path for the reconsideration process and providing a consistent reference point for you and your staff. A materials challenge presents personal and emotional issues for all involved. The community member or parent is deeply concerned about their family having access to certain content or about the library maintaining objectivity; the librarian being questioned is ready to defend their program, their selections, and their patrons' right to read. In contrast, a policy provides a neutral, dispassionate set of expectations that are not subject to the emotions of the moment. Point back to the policy frequently during difficult conversations. For that to be effective, you must review your policy to ensure it supports the vision and desired outcomes of your organization. You will not be surprised that our starting point is, again, your team.

Gathering Team Input

The selection and reconsideration policy and procedures have the potential to touch every employee in your organization. Your team puts theoretical policy into actual daily practice, so their thoughts are vital to developing a workable set of guidelines. Before you communicate with staff about this process, be sure you understand your organization's protocols for updating the policy. Do you have the authority to initiate policy updates or is that up to your governing board? If the latter is the case, can you request a policy audit and recommend changes? Many school boards purchase canned policies. Can you suggest edits to those policies? If changes to the policy are not possible, remember that departmental procedures and guidelines are often simpler to update; use this fact to your advantage to make speedier and more responsive procedural changes. This is also the time to reference the information-gathering you did when you surveyed the landscape. The climate, culture, and frequent conversations in your organization, board, and community will impact how you approach a policy and procedure update with savvy.

Armed with background knowledge, formulate a plan to hear as many staff voices as possible before, during, and after updating the language of your policy and procedure. In the coming chapters, you will identify roles for all staff members in your book challenge action plan, but you should not wait until that stage to involve staff in the planning process. How will you solicit and collect their crucial concerns and needs? Reach out to librarians, pages/assistants, technical staff, directors/principals, and other administrators; anyone who interacts with library users should be privy to the policy and therefore should have input. See the list below for sample questions. Keep in mind that your questions may be shaped by the policy assessment you will read about later in this chapter, and that review may require you to return to staff for additional questioning. Leave flexibility for non-linear processes.

Questions to Ask Your Team Before a Policy Revision

- Have you ever fielded questions from a library user regarding library materials, displays, or programs?
- What kinds of support would be helpful to you when facing such questions?
- Do you know the library's materials selection policy and procedures?
- In what situations have you or would you reference them?
- Considering your role, what would be most useful for you to see in a library selection and reconsideration policy?

Keep communication best practices in mind as you plan for gathering input. Forms and surveys are efficient but impersonal. In-person conversations are time-consuming but provide data points that are not available via a survey: body language, facial expressions, and tone of voice. Conversations also offer the opportunity to request staff members to clarify or expand on their feedback. A combination of surveys and conversation may provide the ideal balance. For example, schedule face-to-face time with a selection of staff and leverage the surveys to poll harder-to-reach individuals whose calendars might make a meeting unrealistic.

The Policy and Procedure Review Team

The size of your policy and procedure review team will vary depending on the size of your organization. In a smaller library, the director may work with just one or two other individuals. We work with our Library Leadership Team, so we have librarians from every level in attendance. When considering who is best suited to do policy review work, draw upon your knowledge of the team's human capital. Call on your analytical teammates who will find cracks and holes in the policy. If no one on your team has raised concerns, find others to ask. Policy creation is too critical to rest on your laurels.

Elements of Policy and Procedure

OIF's "Selection & Reconsideration Policy Toolkit for Public, School, & Academic Libraries" recommends including the following elements in your selection and reconsideration policy and procedures:

Crafting Policies with Confidence: Two Starting Points

The Office for Intellectual Freedom's (OIF) "Selection & Reconsideration Policy Toolkit" is a great place to begin the process of policy revision or creation. It provides areas that should be included in every policy, which is especially helpful if you are writing a policy from scratch. Each organization's policy and procedures will vary; view the considerations through the lens of knowledge specific to your library.

Use this QR code or go to **ala.org/tools/challengesupport/selectionpolicytoolkit** to access OIF's Selection & Reconsideration Policy Toolkit.

You can also reach out to OIF at oif@ala.org to ask for specific policy examples from other libraries. If you are working to develop a specific area of your policy, OIF can provide sample policies that exemplify what you're looking for.

In addition, the Association for Library Service to Children (ALSC) has recently published a helpful "Toolkit for Program Challenges" for creating policies and procedures pertaining to youth services library programs. Use this toolkit to help you craft language regarding programs.

Use this QR code or go to **ala.org/alsc/publications-resources/toolkit-program-challenges** to access the ALSC's Toolkit for Program Challenges.

- Selection
    - Library Mission
    - Intellectual Freedom Statement
    - Objectives
    - Persons Responsible for Selection
    - Selection Criteria
    - Acquisitions Procedures
    - Special Collections
    - Selecting Controversial Materials
    - Gifts and Donations
    - Collection Maintenance and Weeding
    - Policy Revision Timeline

- Reconsideration
    - Reconsideration Procedure
    - Guiding Principles
    - Statement of Policy
    - How to Handle Informal Complaints
    - Request for Formal Reconsideration
    - Sample Reconsideration Form
    - Sample Letter to Complainant
    - Makeup of Reconsideration Committees

Policy or Procedure?

We have seen policies that range in size from brief to quite long. It can be difficult to decide what goes into the policy and what belongs in procedures. While there is no definitive answer that suits all organizations, a general rule of thumb is to put into the policy anything that needs official backing. If a guideline should not have any flexibility, then it should be in the policy. For example, listing the persons responsible for selecting materials will likely be good information to have in the policy. A basic selection criteria statement is important to have in the policy. However, a list of selection resources for librarians may reside in procedures, where it can have the flexibility to be changed easily as publications change over time.

When weighing whether to place information in the policy versus the procedures, considering your intended audience can also be helpful. The policy guides librarians, but it also notably informs the governing board and public. The procedures, while not hidden from the view of the board or public, add detail to the policy specifically for the library team to execute. Take the specifics of dealing with discarded books, for example. While the policy should confirm that responsibility for the weeding and deselection of books rests with librarians, the information on which organizations or recycling programs should receive discarded books can reside in procedures, as this may change more frequently. Ultimately, use your knowledge of your organization, governing board, and community to think through how your policy will or will not support your team. If you sense that the policy may leave your team vulnerable to unmanageable book challenges, err on the side of caution and add more detail to the policy. It may be that your governing board is not supportive of such changes. In either case, add as much strength and guidance as you can to your procedures.

Evaluating the Policy

After collecting input from your colleagues, assess the strengths and weaknesses of your policy and procedures. Examine the areas of your policy that pertain to materials selection, the reconsideration process, protocols for weeding and discarding books, and any other pertinent fields. As a helpful exercise, imagine you have received a challenge and need to launch a reconsideration process per your current policy and procedures. Pay attention to points in them that are unclear or open to interpretation. Note areas that would leave your staff feeling unsupported or confused, referring to your recent survey of staff needs for guidance.

Policy Considerations

Q Does your policy directly reference and affirm intellectual freedom or the Library Bill of Rights as a basis for decision-making?

OIF recommends including a statement of support for intellectual freedom in your board-approved policy. This instantly establishes your organization's commitment to the right to read and expands your policy's point of reference. It does not restrict the library users' right to question materials, but it does confirm that one family's or user's reading preference shall not be binding on other families or users. Furthermore, consider including a statement in your selection policy maintaining that materials should be considered as a whole. When selecting library materials, library professionals must take the entire work into account, and include or exclude it based on the value it would bring to the collection, rather than pulling out particular aspects or passages from the work to justify exclusion.

Q Who can challenge materials?

As your policy is currently written, must a challenger be part of your community? Depending on who your library serves and how your institution is organized, you may want to limit challenges to those who vote to elect your school board members or those who live in the school district attendance area. If you didn't come across such rules when you surveyed the landscape in chapter 2, check into this now by speaking to your organization's legal counsel or other local authority.

Q Does the policy ensure that materials are available to library users while they are being reconsidered?

One's natural instinct might be to pull books from the shelf in the face of an informal or formal inquiry, to set them aside until the matter is resolved. However, your policy's stated dedication to intellectual freedom means that materials should be available to library users unless a formal reconsideration committee deems the materials to be inappropriate for your collection per the selection policy. A hasty book pull, even when done with the best intentions, implies agreement with the concern and denies the material a fair and objective review. Add a clear statement to your policy so materials remain in circulation while the reconsideration process is underway and so library staff can refer back to that requirement to support their actions.

Q Is there a limit on how many times an item can be challenged, or how long a decision to remove or retain an item is binding? And is the decision binding on all libraries in your system?

We recommend that once a material has been reconsidered, the decision to remove or retain the book stands for a period of time without option to reconsider again. For example, your policy could say that the decision of a reconsideration committee is binding for three years, after which it may be considered again. The benefits of this policy include saving your organization from spending time fielding repeated challenges to the same book. On the other side, if a book were removed from circulation, could it be added back after a period of time? Perhaps a librarian or community member could complete a reconsideration request for a team to request reinstatement of the title after three years.

Q Do your policies and procedures differentiate between library materials and curricular materials?

In a school district setting, are your selection and reconsideration policies lumped in with your curriculum policies? This is often the case, but it can put a school library at a disadvantage in the case of a library book challenge, as curricular materials are usually required or recommended for all students in a class or grade. In contrast, the students' choice of library materials should be entirely optional and based on personal preference. This difference greatly impacts the process of the reconsideration committee, which decides whether to keep a library book as an option on the shelf or whether curriculum materials will be taught to a potentially large group of students. If your organization opts to keep library and curricular materials together in the policy, include clear language that outlines the differences between the two types of challenges and make sure that both the library and curriculum departments have solid procedures that further elaborate on the policy.

Q Do you have forms for reconsideration? What do they include?

The OIF toolkit contains a good sample form for reconsideration that you can use or revise for your specific needs. When adopting or creating a form, pay attention to questions about examining the book. OIF's sample includes the following questions: "Have you examined the entire resource? If not, what sections did you review?"

In addition to these questions, consider adding a recommendation or requirement that the complainant read the entire work. As mentioned above, it is essential that library material be considered as a whole piece of writing instead of picking out particular passages. In order to fully assess whether the overall story or message warrants the inclusion of a difficult or graphic passage, the reconsideration committee needs to read the entire work; the questioner should read it for the same reason.

Q   Is the makeup of the reconsideration committee included? How and when will that team come together, and on what criteria will they base their decisions?

When a challenge moves from informal to formal, a reconsideration committee needs to form quickly. Having a ready list of roles to include on the committee helps to hasten the process. The OIF toolkit provides helpful guidelines for reconsideration committees, which should include a combination of members of the school or public library impacted, plus community members and/or administrators from elsewhere in the organization.

Q   Does the policy cap the number of challenges that can be submitted at once or the number that your organization will consider in a year?

Reconsideration policies and procedures often promise official decisions two to four weeks from the submission of the request for reconsideration form. This, however, ranges from challenging to impossible if you receive multiple requests at the same time. Consider including a caveat for multiple requests or a limit on how many requests you will accept at one time. You will also want to require a separate reconsideration form for each title questioned, even if your committee will consider more than one book at a time.

This question points to a very difficult reality: many school districts and library systems are bogged down in multiple challenges, sometimes as many as 100 at a time.[1] Aim to find a balance between efficiency for your team, timeliness for the challenger, and thoroughness for a thoughtful outcome.

Q   Do your policies and procedures include considerations for library displays or programs?

To strengthen your library's response to such questions, your selection policy should affirm the librarian's authority to select materials for displays based on their professional judgment of patron interest, community happenings, representation of diverse cultures and identities, and more. At the same time, a public library should address the content of its programming. Programs that are completely optional for children, families, and adults means that libraries will not restrict these programs from any users who wish to attend them. In addition, the library will seek to address the interests of a wide range of patrons in its programming. On the school side, your organization may want to provide advance notification to families when programs such as authors' visits will take place during the school day. Alternatively, these events can be held after school so families may opt in. Whatever the case, think ahead about how to avoid a last-minute cancellation with a contracted author.

Navigating Uncertainty: The Consequences of Ambiguous or Missing Policies

When patrons questioned the displays at a local public library, library assistants found themselves caught in the crossfire. One rotating display shelf held options of LGBTQ+ titles for adults, and another historical installation presented images of Black figures from the Civil Rights Movement on large banners. While the library's policy had clear processes for the reconsideration of library materials, library displays were not addressed in the policy. As is often the case, library assistants fielded questions from heated patrons. This was a stressful moment for the part-time staff who were not sure how to respond. Fortunately, the assistants referred the patrons to the library director, who could address the question.

Had the library's policy addressed displays directly, staff would have been able to point back to the policy as the bedrock for their decisions. However, simply having the policy on the books would not be useful without clear training for all staff on the library's collection development policies. In addition, scripts and designated roles for all library staffers would relieve their anxiety at not knowing what or how much to say to an angry patron.

Use this QR code or go to **alaeditions.org/webextras** to access the Policy Considerations Worksheet, which includes the questions in this section as a downloadable, editable worksheet.

What's Next?

Take your policy and procedure recommendations back through your team or a smaller sample of your workforce, such as a leadership team. Ask them to find any areas that raise questions or concerns. Once your policy and procedures are solid, it is time to create a game plan and build your team's capacity to carry it out. The rest of your preparation plan rests on the soundness of your foundational documents. Take time to review and strengthen your policy and procedures.

CHRONICLE YOUR JOURNEY!

Which voices from your team have you heard from most in this process so far? Who has not yet had the opportunity to share input? How will you include them?

_____

_____

_____

_____

Based on the policy evaluation considerations above, which areas of your selection and reconsideration policies and procedures need attention?

_____

_____

_____

_____

After reading this chapter, what ideas, questions, or action steps do you want to use to inform your work as you delve into policy evaluation and revision or creation with your team?

_____

_____

_____

_____

NOTE

1. American Library Association, "American Library Association Releases Preliminary Data on 2023 Book Challenges," news release, September 19, 2023, www.ala.org/news/press-releases/2023/09/american-library-association-releases-preliminary-data-2023-book-challenges.

PART II

WORDS INTO ACTION
Operationalizing the Challenge Response Action Plan

Having concluded part I with its focus on policies for addressing a challenge, much of the work in part II is designed to prepare your team for the precursor to a challenge, the inquiry. Even a laundry list of titles targeted for removal begins as an inquiry, although perhaps not one directed at the library's professional staff. The result of the work outlined in part II is a "response action plan." In the work, teams begin to explore the nuances, hidden pitfalls, and their comfort as individuals carrying out the directives of the library's policies. As team members apply what had been theoretical, their relationships continue to benefit from carefully structured work, recognizing the toll exacted by its intensity. For this reason, we dive deeply and continually into the work of strengthening team relationships.

CHAPTER 4

Readying Your Team for Cohesive Action

The work of establishing a response action plan begins with training all staff members on your foundational policies and procedures. While some of your staff members may have been involved in the previous development work, for others it will be new, making this step critical. The amount of time devoted to team training depends on the size of your organization. Do not overlook this step; it is just as likely that an initial inquiry or communication about a challenge will come to a shelving page or desk clerk as to the library professional on the reference desk. Everyone in the organization needs to have some familiarity with the policies in place and the procedures guiding them as they hand off the inquiry in a professional manner to the appropriate colleague.

You should launch the training with conversations about policies and procedures at management team meetings, staff meetings, and during professional development days. It is possible that several leaders will share this content and lead these conversations. When multiple individuals are leading training, do not proceed until the presenters have a common understanding of the implications of the policies and procedures. Any mixed or conflicting messages at this stage spread confusion and can complicate implementation in a manner that damages team relationships and puts the smooth implementation of the response at risk. Spend as much time reviewing the policies and procedures with the leadership team as necessary to ensure unity.

As your team works through the policies and procedures, listen carefully to questions, comments, side conversations, and observe body language. These behaviors convey signals that allow you to assess your team's readiness to plan for and respond to challenges in a unified manner. It is important to carefully consider how to respond to any signs of anxiety or disagreement. Some of your team will be comfortable voicing their questions or concerns, while others will struggle to express their apprehension even when speaking one-on-one. Now is the time to deploy every listening skill at your disposal. You need to hear what is being said. Most likely if one team member has a question or concern, others do as well. Managing inquiries and challenges means facing conflict and difficult situations; very few people are comfortable with those circumstances. For this reason, it is critical that solid preparation includes practice and scripted language to serve as a guide.

To illustrate this point, when leading a meeting, if you observe a team member rolling their eyes, shifting their chair away from a colleague, or changing the focus of the conversation, that is a red flag. These types of actions signal discomfort with the content or annoyance with the speaker. You may decide to ask an invitational question such as, "Henry, how are you feeling about this procedure? Is it clear? Do you feel your team at the circulation desk will be able to manage this piece?" Similarly, you may observe a team member turning their head away while muttering under their breath. Based on your knowledge of the individual, you may simply make a mental note to engage with them individually outside the meeting. One way to begin a conversation of this type would be, "Sarah, it seemed like when we were discussing X, you disagreed or had questions about how that could work. Is there a concern you have or is there an aspect of our plan that is missing? Can you share what that discomfort is about?" Either of these choices provides opportunities to invite into the conversation anyone who may have a concern to raise but is unsure of how it will be received.

These examples of observing and positively engaging with colleagues build trust, signaling that it is okay to have questions or discomfort. The invitations also model how you want your leaders to be engaging with their own teams. This is how cohesive teams are built. It takes time, patience, and a willingness to backtrack and make repairs to relationships. It is easy to miss a cue or respond superficially where the behavior reveals that further engagement and attention are required.

Once training on policies and procedures is deployed to the wider team, continue to attend to how team members engage with each other and the content. Plan opportunities for personal reflection, sharing reflections with a small group of colleagues, asking for clarification, or providing feedback. Some aspects of the work may cause anxiety. Some team members may need time to process the content and professional implications privately before sharing with a leader or colleague, particularly if sharing will happen in a large group setting. Assess team preparedness with direct conversations. This work cannot be done effectively with e-mail memos from an office. It requires face-to-face conversations with team members at all levels of the organization's operations.

Prepare your team for this demanding work by establishing or strengthening clear norms for meeting conduct and collegial support. This allows staff to bring their genuine concerns to the group without fear of ridicule or being thought less professional than their peers. It also provides a framework for practicing the types of engagement and behavior that are expected when managing an inquiry.

As action plans develop, have your team work to calmly discuss potential challenges and their management. Negative and insulting comments about the individuals bringing an inquiry, whether actual community members or ones invented in a role-playing scenario, should be discouraged. It is tough to break out of a defensive or combative mindset when faced with a real inquiry. The point of the practice is to alleviate some of the negative feelings for the professional communicating with the community member, and thus make achieving a mutually beneficial outcome possible.

Establishing Psychological Safety for the Team

Your staff brings a variety of beliefs, opinions, and emotions to this work. You need to create an environment that recognizes and allows for those differences and doesn't leave any team members feeling vulnerable, pressured, or isolated.

Effective Communication: Sample Language for Team Check-ins

- How comfortable would you be discussing our policies with a library user?
- What do you see as your role in addressing community inquiries?
- What supporting documentation or information would you need?
- Is there a point in the process where you would no longer feel confident leading the conversation?
- What pitfalls do you anticipate?
- What are your concerns personally and professionally?
- What additional training would increase your confidence in carrying out our policies and procedures?

This can be overwhelming and is ongoing work that demands careful attention. Without requiring team members to share all the details of their circumstances, be aware that there will be economic and psychological elements dictating what some individuals are able to offer. All team members need to recognize that the constraints are not indicative of that person's dedication to the organization, the library users, or the mission of libraries. Key elements in establishing this safety for your team include building trust, cultivating inclusion, and providing space for collegial sharing and support.

Building Trust

Building trust is the essence of this work; however, it will not be important to any of your team members unless you demonstrate its importance to you. This means dedicating time, attention, and resources to ensure it is not neglected. The behavior of your leadership team members throughout this work must model an openness to discomfort, strong emotions, and uncertainty. Your ability to learn and be vulnerable plays a large part in building trust with the team members who will play a part in addressing inquiries and challenges.

Cultivating Inclusion

You can use questions to lead planning conversations while drawing your team together. When only the leadership team or a handful of staff are engaged in the conversation, concerns may be overshadowed and gaps in planning might be overlooked. To ensure that all staff have an opportunity to process and respond to policies, procedures, and the action plan, it is necessary to provide a variety of avenues for soliciting input. Remember, not every staff member will be comfortable speaking up in the group, particularly if they have a concern or question that contrasts with those of more vocal team members.

Providing Space

Intentionally hold back and allow space for team members to respond and support each other when discussing procedures and action plans. Pausing before diving in with a response provides an opening for the team to support its members from within. This type of internal bonding increases ownership of the final plan and builds trust between you and your team, as well as among team members.

Capacity to Respond

As team members internalize this training, they may assume that their colleagues are reacting and planning in a manner that reflects their own, but individual circumstances vary. Experienced team members are likely aware of the commitment, risks, and rewards of addressing challenges. Other team members may be surprised at the intense focus the work demands. Because responding to challenges can be risky, and may involve drawing media attention and, more recently, even personal targeting and threats, not all of your library team members will be comfortable engaging in the more public-facing tasks. There are additional factors that could impact individual team members' capacity to respond, including being:

- A sole income earner
- A caregiver to children and/or adults
- Deeply uncomfortable with conflict
- Fearful of public exposure
- Triggered by past trauma

Library managers need to be aware of but do not need to know the details of these situations as they impact team members. It is awareness of the existence of these concerns that is relevant when selecting the response team.

Managers also need to be aware that there may well be underlying influences affecting the degree of confidence their team members have in engaging in this work. The best way to gauge a team member's confidence is to ask them. If they are not confident in fulfilling the responsibilities being planned for their role in the organization, leaders can ask if they would like more support or if their personal circumstances prevent them from fulfilling that role. If they are not able to fulfill the role for personal reasons, there will be plenty of work to be done that does not require direct engagement in contentious situations or public-speaking appearances that would leave them feeling at risk.

What is gained from considering team members' capacity is the ability to anticipate and avoid the internal conflicts that arise when colleagues make assumptions about implementing the plan. Experienced team members may expect all of their colleagues to rally to the cause with intensity. As was explored earlier, potential reluctance on an individual's part may simply reflect their personal circumstances and not be at all reflective of their dedication to the library's mission. When the external and very real constraints are known, this allows for effective backup plans should a designated staff member not be available when their role needs to be activated. Plans B, C, and D are beautiful safety nets to have in place, particularly in stressful situations.

The outcomes of the conversations that take place in safe spaces allow you to select the team members best qualified and best suited to serve on the library's response team.

Preparatory Training

Ensure that all team members have the proper training to execute their role. Clerical staff need to be provided with the basic premises of intellectual freedom and the corresponding policies. This is not training to prepare them to respond in an official capacity, but so they can knowledgeably communicate with library users and community members about where inquiries should be directed. It will help them avoid making false or confusing statements based on their own misperceptions about the library's mission and organizational values.

One way to build strong team relationships and provide background knowledge is to create discussion groups that include the staff from a variety of roles.

The Playbill Perspective: Inspiration from a Theater Troupe

Included in the playbill of a local theater was a page sharing the troupe's values. The contributions encompassed all of the staff and were used not only to drive a season opening orientation, but were made public for all of their audiences. This type of transparency is an indicator of a serious commitment to upholding these shared values and reflected the investment of the entire staff. It provides a solid model for establishing commitment on library teams as well.

The values in the playbill included but were not limited to clear, honest communication, taking personal responsibility, and believing there is always more to learn. Each commitment articulated the values of the team. These values were shared with each other, agreed upon, made public, and served as a touchstone for maintaining the relationships reflecting the true, best intentions of the entire team. Documents like this are important. They refocus and unify teams in times of stress.

Do not underestimate the potential negative impact of an offhand comment by a facilities worker or a shelving page. It is often difficult for library users and community members to distinguish between support and professional staff. Everyone needs to understand the mission of the library, the purpose of the collection, and how to manage inquiries from the community.

Anticipate and Address Conflict

There will be conflict within your team. It may start small, with impatience expressed over a colleague's question during a meeting. Often the tiny annoyance that is present at the very start of conflict is overlooked, since it is easier to ignore it than to engage in a confrontation. It is rare for individuals to be trained in constructively addressing workplace frustrations. But over time these minor irritations can fester and lead to growing anger and resentment. Doing the work to get ahead of these situations can normalize responding with care and consideration internally, while providing an example of the practice that will serve the entire organization should an external challenge arise.

We experience conflict every day, in and out of our workplace. We even experience our own self-generated internal conflicts. The big challenge is knowing when conflict is fleeting and when it has the potential to fester and become a full-blown catastrophe. Along the continuum of conflict, ignoring it is rarely the answer. An early proactive response to conflict allows it to be used to your advantage.

Work to normalize the initial indicators of conflict, emphasizing that conflict will happen and is not an indicator to launch hostilities. Conflict is an indicator that change is needed. The change could mean altering a process, shifting a goal, making a change to staff assignments, or undertaking some relationship work. All of this work is necessary to ensure the team is united and prepared to face external pressure.

Listen to your team's conversations and identify the "broken record" issues (i.e., "I don't think X is who we should have speaking to the media!"). These are the hot buttons that may seem minor but can escalate into resentment. In a similar vein, teach your library staff to listen for the "broken record" issues among library users and community members, providing insight into challenges that can flare up seemingly from nowhere.

Have a plan for addressing a misstep by a team member. People make mistakes. Perhaps an off-the-cuff comment is made in a public space. Maybe a rash e-mail is fired off in the heat of the moment. Keep in mind that these types of complications can happen, and plan to address them. As challenging as it can be, assume that no harm was intended, and the staffer's action was perhaps ill-planned but not malicious. Directly and privately discuss the action and the fallout with the individual team member. Explore possible actions to mitigate the damage. Plan how to address the error with the larger team, recognizing that mistakes will be made, and determine how to recover as a team.

You need to take all of these components for building team relationships and use them specifically to carry out policies and procedures addressing intellectual freedom challenges. Carry them with you as we move into designing an action plan and assigning roles for using that plan in the face of a community challenge.

PART II | Words into Action

CHRONICLE YOUR JOURNEY!

What commitments will you make to your team?

_____

_____

What commitments will they need to make to each other?

_____

_____

What assumptions are you making about your team's cohesiveness?

_____

_____

How do team members with differing professional responsibilities interact?

_____

_____

How will your schedules, meetings, and training change in order to allow for a more unified work environment?

_____

_____

As you launch this work, what professional experiences can you share to begin conversations about the work necessary to become a challenge-ready team?

_____

_____

CHAPTER 5

Designing and Launching an Action Plan

As you embark on designing and launching an action plan, it will be important to keep in mind that the resulting demands on your team take place alongside rather than instead of normal day-to-day operations. The work of establishing a challenge-ready team intersects with the normal development of a cohesive library team as they carry out their daily responsibilities and address snags that occur in any workplace.

Daily operations will continue throughout this demanding work. Maintaining balance in all areas of operation is tricky, requiring careful attention and flexibility. You should anticipate complications and delays, so when the circulation system goes down on the day a planning meeting was scheduled, you will have the capacity to adapt the timeline without losing momentum.

Leaders should strive to embed the plan's implementation fully into the workplace culture; the meetings and training support the staff's internalization of the concepts, processes, and mindset for addressing challenges. The experience of building a cohesive team is beneficial when similar work is undertaken throughout the organization with all manner of processes, policies, and procedures. The unity of the team is beneficial beyond the preparation for a challenge. Ideally, the structure implemented here will become embedded in daily practice. A team fully immersed in this work evolves into a team prepared for any upheaval or difficult circumstances impacting the organization.

Were this training and implementation undertaken only after an initial inquiry had been raised, the result would likely be a mad scramble to respond. Unpreparedness amplifies reactive and emotional responses, leaving the door open for internal strife, hasty mistakes, and public missteps. There is no library, regardless of size, that is immune to divisive issues around some aspect of its service. To hope that you will not experience this type of stress within your organization is unrealistic. Therefore, planning for this eventuality represents an essential management practice.

Building an Action Plan

Your action plan must identify the team members who will be actively involved in responding to an inquiry or challenge, and create a communication plan for their response to an inquiry.

Identifying the Response Team

Action plans are reliant on the understanding and investment of the team members responsible for their implementation. For that reason, the careful selection of individuals to carry out the work of addressing inquiries and challenges is integral to the plan's successful execution. The scope of your plan and the size of your organization dictate the number of staff members who will be directly and actively engaged in this work. Mapping out the roles to be filled, and reflecting on the capacity of your team members to meet those demands with confidence, is well worth the time and effort, as this will ensure that your plan is carried out as intended.

To begin this work, consider and identify the individual(s) to whom an external inquiry should be reported at both the branch or school level and within the larger department. For example, an inquiry received by a shelving page may first be reported to the certified library professional supervising at the time of the inquiry. That individual may then report to the branch supervisor, the department supervisor, and/or the library director.

Along this pathway, it is vital to communicate who will respond to the inquirer, and the acceptable time frame within which they will be contacted to further explore the concern being raised. Depending on the staffing of the library at the time of the inquiry, it may be possible to respond immediately; however, it is more likely to be necessary to collect contact information from the inquirer to share it with the appropriate professional.

With a pathway in mind, identify the team member(s):
- Who will assume responsibility for communicating with the library user/community member
- Who will need to be notified and kept updated
- Who will be talking with lawyers
- Who will be speaking to the media

Consider these criteria for individual team members; that is, their
- Professional role
- Level of experience
- Level of training
- Individual comfort with difficult conversations
- Availability

Identifying the response team members may involve some trial and error. Assigning roles and managing the flow of actions necessary for addressing an inquiry or challenge hinges on individuals' abilities and disposition. Take into consideration the degree to which their abilities are trusted by other team members. This is one of several stages where the early work of laying a foundation of trust among your team members will pay off in a more effective process.

Create a Communication Pathway

You should create a flowchart, like the one shown in figure 5.1, of the various roles necessary to respond to an inquiry or challenge as it progresses along the pathway provided by the library's policies and procedures. Pair the roles in the flowchart with individuals based on an assessment of their professional attributes and the demands their responsibilities will make on them.

Library organizations range in size from one professional to a staff of hundreds. The larger the organization, the more difficult it is to have a clear pathway for addressing concerns. The need for clear communication will be discussed in detail in later chapters, but developing the flowchart for relaying and responding to an inquiry is of the utmost importance. While the pathway may be short and direct in smaller organizations, their work in creating a flowchart of supporters and library champions will be quite similar and equally important to that of larger organizations.

Ideally, a professionally trained librarian close to the point of service for the inquirer responds to the inquiry. Proximity provides a level of connection, smoothing the conversational pathway and allowing the inquirer to feel heard. In addition, proximity allows for a timely response that is not possible if the identified responder is not directly assigned to the school or branch receiving the inquiry. This type of connection and timely response provides conditions more favorable for a calm response than the feeling of defensiveness or elusiveness that results from delaying or moving the conversation up the organization chart at an early stage in the process. The careful preparation of the whole team to utilize the flowchart benefits the organization as multiple individuals contribute to addressing inquiries appropriately.

FIGURE 5.1

Communication pathway for inquiry responses

01

Inquiry received by **Response Team** member – proceed to Step 2

Inquiry received by **Non-Response Team** member – pass to Response team colleague – proceed to Step 2

Engage in **informal conversation** with inquirer to seek to schedule meeting to address concerns

02

03

Use the scheduled meeting to:
- fully explore the concern
- share insights into collection development
- discuss specific content concerns
- share and explore potential solutions

Explain reconsideration process if necessary

04

Do not overlook the need to make time to connect with partners outside of the immediate library operations. Trustees, members of city government, or district administrators should all be made aware of the policy, procedures, and the communication flowchart. This not only makes a prompt and accurate response more likely, but it also helps prevent elected or appointed officials from overstepping their authority while failing to follow organizational policy.

Take a Moment for Clarity and Consistency

Inquiries will arrive at unpredictable times. The library staff needs to follow the communication pathway as closely as possible. When it is not immediately possible for a non-response team member to redirect an inquiry, there are steps that can be taken to alleviate the pressure to respond.

Scheduling Conversations

A timely response conveys a sense of preparedness and competence. This assumes that the inquiry is directed at a team member who is equipped to respond directly. However, if the frontline responder is not trained or authorized to address inquiries or is experiencing an emotional response to the inquiry, it is wise to delay an in-depth conversation, or make a referral to a colleague while support and resources are gathered.

The ideal is to respond to an inquiry by gathering basic information regarding the concern, and then requesting to schedule a conversation for further discussion when the team member is not subject to distractions or the demands of other responsibilities. Scheduling a second conversation is constructive for both parties. A scheduled conversation allows everyone involved to identify the concerns that need to be addressed and gather the information and resources needed to respond effectively. It can also reduce the emotions resulting from both the inquirer's mustering the courage to raise a concern and from the frontline responder's feeling of being caught off guard when the concern is delivered.

The Challenge Response Team's Action Plan

Develop a "rollout framework" to map your action plan, like the one in table 5.1. You should maintain this chart and track your progress through its steps, adapting them to address any oversights as they are identified.

With the response team, communication pathway, and a strategic response action plan in place, all team members need to practice, internalizing the process by revisiting inquiries others may have experienced and rehearsing scenarios with scripted language to support the development of honed responses. It is also important to anticipate the need for updates and retraining. This work is important when managing staff attrition and the onboarding of new team members, and must not be isolated from those circumstances.

Use this QR code or go to **alaeditions.org/webextras** to access the Challenge-Ready Action Plan Rollout Framework, a downloadable and editable version of table 5.1.

TABLE 5.1
Rollout framework for a challenge-ready action plan

Purpose: Implementation of the Library Challenge Response Plan to provide a consistent message for all team members.

RESPONDER	ACTION	COMPLETE
Library Leadership	Develop or update Selection & Reconsideration (S&R) policies.	☐
Library Leadership	Script the introduction of S&R policies to the governing body.	☐
Library Leadership	Submit the S&R policies for adoption, as needed.	☐
Library Leadership	Provide the S&R policies to all team members and alert them to upcoming training for implementation.	☐
Library Leadership	Plan intentional, ongoing conversations about confidentiality, discretion, and awareness of the impact of public conversations for *every* staff and volunteer team member.	☐
Library Leaders	Meet with the library leadership team to introduce an action plan for implementing the S&R policies and procedures.	☐
Library Leadership	Identify roles for library team members who will have an active and visible role in addressing inquiries and challenges.	☐
Library Leadership	Reach a consensus on the action plan's implementation and have a unified approach before rolling out the plan in whole-team training.	☐
Library Leadership	Design the rollout out of the action plan to the full team.	☐
Library Leadership/ Dept. Leaders	Meet with the individuals identified as having an active and visible role in receiving and addressing inquiries and challenges; listen for hesitancy and/or any need for training support on their part; and check for their understanding of their role and confidence in their ability to meet expectations.	☐
Library Leadership	Carry out departmental training, allowing for feedback, disagreement, and conversation.	☐
Library Leadership	Outline and share a schedule for review, practice, reflection, and revision of the action plan to be carried out by departments and at whole-team training.	☐
Library Leadership	Normalize conversations about inquiries, questions, and suggestions introduced by internal and external members of the library community.	☐
Library Leadership	Plan to transition from the rollout of the action plan to ongoing maintenance and awareness of the action plan.	☐
	Add additional steps as identified for your unique organization.	
		☐
		☐

Table 5.2 provides a sample framework for both onboarding new team members and maintaining the staff's awareness of the action plan (and intellectual freedom issues) over time.

Use this QR code or go to **alaeditions.org/webextras** to access the Ongoing Plan for Onboarding and Refreshing, a downloadable and editable version of table 5.2.

TABLE 5.2
Ongoing training plan for team onboarding and maintaining action plan awareness

Purpose: Establish ongoing professional development for all team members in order to normalize conversations and onboard members consistently.

INITIATOR	ACTION	COMPLETE
Library Leadership	Review the Selection & Reconsideration (S&R) policies annually.	☐
Library Leadership	Update the S&R policies and submit them for adoption as needed.	☐
Library Leadership	Provide the up-to-date S&R policies in the library team's onboarding packet along with the long-range plan, goals, and other policies and procedures.	☐
Library Leadership	Facilitate ongoing conversations with library staff about the importance of confidentiality, discretion, and the need for awareness of the impact of public conversations.	☐
Library Leaders	Plan *interdepartmental* conversations to maintain awareness of action plan procedures, share experiences, and understand the expectations of all team members.	☐
Leadership Team (Managers/Leads)	Monitor professional publications to inform conversations, and share with staff at meetings, in newsletters, via social media, in organizational chat, etc.	☐
Team Members	Monitor conversations within the library and community, documenting their concerns for the library leadership.	☐
Team Members	Be intentional in collection development work, and recognize that being able to articulate the value and purpose of selected materials is critical to this work.	☐
Team Members	Develop and sustain library services/programming to educate the community about issues pertaining to intellectual freedom.	☐
Leadership Team Members	Share observations, efforts, and professional resources in order to remain alert to trends within the wider educational/library community.	☐
Library Leadership	Preserve time during regular team meetings to touch on issues of intellectual freedom, and tie this to goals in the library organization's long-range plan.	☐
Add additional steps as identified for your unique organization.		
		☐
		☐
		☐

Being Solo without Being Alone

If you are a solo librarian, all the responsibility for responding rests with you as the library manager. In a community with a solo librarian, it is just as likely that an inquiry will come to a shelving page, a volunteer, or a member of the custodial staff as to the professional. Often in smaller communities, conversations of this nature happen in community spaces. For example, casual conversations can shift into inquiries while in line at the coffee shop or walking in a park. Having everyone on staff be aware of the established processes and their role in referring these inquiries to you is critical to effectively addressing the inquiry.

By the same token, solo librarians need to draw on resources within the community: their board of trustees or board of education, colleagues in schools or public libraries, or perhaps local bookstore owners. These allies can provide essential support in defending against a challenge. The range of circumstances are numerous; therefore, we have designed this content to be adaptable to your unique situation.

CHRONICLE YOUR JOURNEY!

Once you have developed a fully realized team process for handling a challenge, how will that look?

_____

_____

_____

How will that team process feel for you and the library management team?

_____

_____

_____

How do you want it to feel for your team members?

_____

_____

_____

PART II | Words into Action

What action steps will help you complete that process?

_____

_____

How will the process be maintained once it has been implemented to ensure that it remains an effective process over time?

_____

_____

_____

Where is your team along the continuum from starting to develop a response team structure to having a training response team in place?

_____

_____

_____

What challenges are you and your team facing in moving this work forward?

_____

_____

_____

What has been the impact of this work on the team's relationships?

_____

_____

_____

CHAPTER 6

Establishing and Training for a Resolution Mindset

With the development of a united team, conflict mediation and management were addressed. As the team coalesces, opportunities to develop the skills needed to successfully execute the work are necessary. Training the team in courageous conversations and conflict management strategies equips them to minimize the negative impact of both internal and external strife. As the whole team acquires a constructive conflict mindset, the focus shifts to supporting response team members who are engaging in frontline communication with library users and community members regarding inquiries and challenges.

Delineating the calm and efficient mindset that staff members should strive to maintain when approached with an inquiry is critical in preventing an emotional exchange from becoming hostile. An early negative interaction immediately puts the library, as an organization, on the defensive. You should train all staff members to respond with curiosity and questions when interacting with inquiries. Designated response team members need to try to understand the inquirer's concerns in a manner like that used to address any patron reference request. The responding staff essentially launch a reference interview to determine the origin of the inquiry, how it is impacting the inquirer, and what their expectations are for addressing the issue. The information shared guides the continuation of the exchange and ideally becomes shared problem-solving. This approach also gives the responding librarian an opportunity to explain the library's mission and modify the library user's experience, without impacting the experience of other library users and community members.

Outline a Plan of Action

You can build a plan of action in outline form, like the one below, to guide and support library team members when they receive an initial inquiry, when that inquiry becomes a challenge, and when they must respond to members outside of the community.

Addressing an Initial Inquiry

- Acknowledge the right of inquirers to express concerns and make individual choices.
- Problem-solve to generate and discuss alternative solutions, thus addressing inquirers' concerns without progressing to a challenge.
- Share resources and strategies that can support meeting patrons' needs (i.e., notes on student accounts, providing alternative reading lists, sharing insights into your organization's mission).
- Balance service demands (balancing parental requests versus student autonomy, and individual library users' needs versus those of the community).
- Avoid demonizing the individual bringing the inquiry, even to yourself.
- Train on and employ conflict resolution strategies.
- Recognize that there are limits to all this. Prepare to manage the emotional impact on individual responders and the team if their initial responses are not successful in addressing the inquirers' concerns.

When an Inquiry Becomes a Challenge

- Activate the policies and procedures that have been formally adopted by your organization.
- Strive to continue interacting with the inquirer in a professional, direct manner.
- Communicate to team members that an escalation in the inquiry is *not* a reflection on the quality of their service or their execution of their responsibilities.

Note: Particularly in the current volatile times, there are often limits to what you and your team can do to avoid having the inquiry proceed to a formal challenge.

When an Inquiry Comes from Outside Your Community

- If forced onto a bigger stage as the target of extreme political organizations, your team will need support and acknowledgment of the inquiry's impact on their well-being.
- You can utilize employee assistance resources to bolster team members as they continue to deliver a calm, efficient, and unified response while carrying out their daily work.
- Draw on the internal relationships of your unified library team to manage the demands on their mental well-being. The team provides a safe space for processing the stress and negative impact of public challenges. It is important to mitigate the isolation of individual team members who are struggling with anger, frustration, and fear.
- Bring in support from outside of the team and organization. There are many resources that can provide guidance and comfort when libraries are facing challenges. Draw on professional organizations and your

collegial network. It is important that you and your team members do not lose contact with the many members of their communities, both personal and professional. Join in bearing witness to the devastation that is increasingly being experienced in our country's libraries.

You should work through these actions and approaches with your response team members. When they have been honed to meet the needs of your response team, share them with all staff members. Every member of the library staff needs to be invested in developing suitable customer service dispositions, as well as being prepared for the emotional impact of this work. Enable your entire team to unite in supporting and understanding the experience of their colleagues who are directly engaged in responding to the inquiry or challenge. Strong support from within the organization is vital to maintaining the well-being of individual staff members and the entire team when facing external stressors.

Meeting Demands with Diplomacy

The sheer number of challenges being brought and intentionally made news by politically motivated organizations has heightened awareness across the spectrum of community members. As a result of this increased awareness, librarians are likely to find themselves addressing more questions from parents, patrons, and citizens. These inquiries are driven by concern and curiosity rather than the more destructive motives of the extremist groups.

While difficult, work with your team to distinguish between the targeted attacks and the information-seeking inquiries. Information-seeking, community-based inquiries can be opportunities, as they are coming from people who are willing to engage in conversation. These interactions can be satisfying and productive. Enable library users to hear and learn about intellectual freedom as a professional area of expertise and about the critical role libraries are meant to play in society. It is in engaging with this segment of the community that the team's investment of time, energy, and emotion in training pays off.

You can continue team development with exercises that stretch your team members' thinking using reflective prompts, such as this one from the respected conflict mediator Tammy Lenski: "If the impossible were possible, what would that look like?"

Encourage your team to imagine successfully addressing an overwhelming and openly hostile challenge from a large extremist organization. What would be necessary to make that happen? In situations where there has been some degree of success, outcomes often hinge on the support of the community. Learn more about those strategies and what it would mean to adapt them in your library community.

Close monitoring of the news about banned book conflicts can provide a healthy awareness of what to actively avoid doing when responding to conflict. Recently an officer in a professional association "liked" a crude post on social media targeting an extremist group and their activities. While the desire to respond in this way is understandable, the reporting of the incident in the media harms the image of both the librarian in their professional capacity and the library as an institution. This is tricky ground to walk, but engaging with anything other than the agreed-upon strategies can be detrimental to the cause. This work is emotionally draining. Monitoring the news can be demoralizing, and while planning for an effective response can be empowering, it is crucial that library leadership attends to the team's well-being. Sharing openly with colleagues helps team members process their emotions and builds the relationships that will sustain them should they face similar circumstances.

All this planning and rehearsing results in a united team that will respond to external challenges and stress with calm efficiency. One of the reactions that the more calculating of challengers count on is having rattled the organization. In the resulting flurry of emotions, mistakes are easily made and weaknesses revealed. Diligent, intentional, careful nurturing and team-building will foil that plan, weakening the challenger's impact. This is the precise moment when having clear, concrete, and concise policies in place is invaluable. Your team and your challengers will have nowhere to go but by the book.

Prepping an "Always On" Team

Inquiries and challenges do not come at convenient times. The resulting stress can cause emotional upheaval among your staff. That means it is important to support library staff in maintaining their personal well-being, thus allowing them to respond with consistency while constructively managing their emotions. The library should have a structure solidly in place that allows team members to balance the demands of their personal and professional lives.

In the life of any organization, there are times when the workload is heavier due to the operations cycle of the library. If there are new initiatives, they need to be calculated into the demands impacting the ability of an individual to respond calmly and constructively to a potential challenge. Your awareness of these factors and the embedded process helps with managing them efficiently and minimizes their negative impact on individuals and the organization.

Responding to Individuals' Emotional Reactions

Encouraging team members to pause and assess their emotions and frame of mind when engaging with an inquiry at work can provide the space to manage these reactions before they escalate and result in negative outcomes. When responding to an inquiry, the team member should:
- Be flexible/adaptable
- Be reflective
- Avoid being defensive
- Know when to lean on others

The pause during the initial phone conversation with an inquirer is often the most significant moment in an exchange. It is the tipping point toward problem-solving and relationship-building and away from animosity. There is every chance that it will prevent an escalation into a formal inquiry and challenge. The ability of

---

Customer Service Dispositions to Keep in Mind

Support all team members in focusing their efforts to always deliver high-quality customer service, so that these dispositions become ingrained. Having a patron-centered mindset provides a safety net when team emotions may run high. Begin with a focus on:
- Listening to student/patron perspectives
- Acting in an equitable manner
- Ensuring ease of access to materials
- Protecting individuals' right to read

You can build the team's comfort with difficult conversations in all areas.

each team member to maintain awareness of their own reactions and manage their own responses is always of immeasurable value, most particularly when under the heightened pressure of a challenge to intellectual freedom.

Mapping Actions to Reduce Emotional Reactions

Having planned and practiced them, incorporating predictable response guidelines is useful in mitigating emotional responses. The "Communication pathway for inquiry responses" flowchart (figure 5.1), combined with the "Staff organization chart for inquiry responses" (figure 6.1), provides a structure for establishing that predictability for your team. It is this type of system response that enables your staff members to feel connected to one another and allows them to pause an exchange and enact the processes they trained on, and which are embedded in organizational practice.

FIGURE 6.1

Staff organization chart for inquiry responses

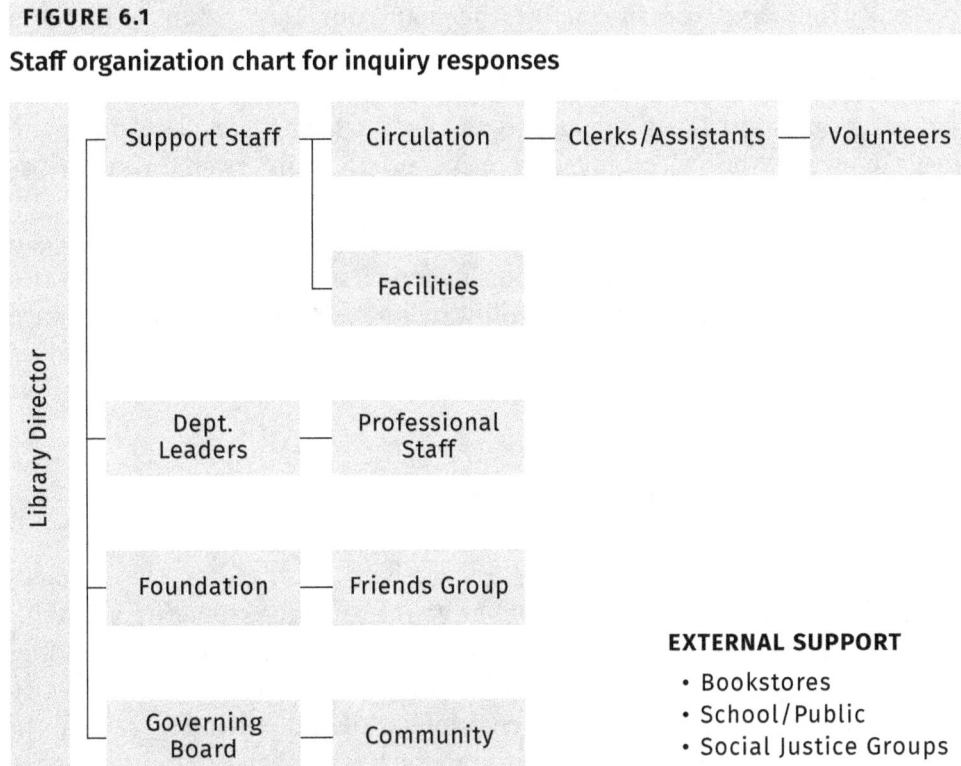

You can expand on the "Communication pathway for inquiry responses" chart by using your organization's staff chart to map action steps tied to specific roles and responsibilities (as shown in figure 6.1). This work must encompass all staff members, as an inquiry can come to a volunteer or shelving page as easily as to the professional staffing the reference desk.

All team members must know both who to alert should they be approached with an inquiry and the basic response actions of gathering contact information and relaying the next steps in the process, which can be as limited as asking the individual to wait while another staff member joins the conversation. For example, a volunteer may alert a colleague at the circulation desk who will then collect contact information, perhaps ask a follow-up question or two, and then relay the inquiry to a member of the library leadership team. Effectively managing inquiries hinges on everyone understanding the process and knowing who is responsible for action steps. This is the foundation that allows for a strategic response and for the library as an organization to present a unified front capable of addressing concerns and mitigating escalation.

Harnessing Emotions for Unity

The effectiveness of the response plan is entirely dependent on training, practice, and rehearsals. The immediate, visceral reaction to an inquiry increases your heart rate and makes your stomach sink, and will also shut your brain down. Practice and scripted rehearsals can provide continuity, calmness, and an ability to manage initial inquiries in a manner that maintains relationships. All of these efforts make coming to a mutually satisfactory outcome and meeting user and community needs while maintaining the mission of the library more likely. To that end, you should focus on practice scenarios, rehearsing, and scripting language to prepare the welcoming, supportive, attentive library staff you want as your front-facing team.

Rehearsal, repetition, and reflection are confidence-boosting tools. You can draw on authentic experiences to demonstrate how scripting language increases the effectiveness of the conversation. Allow individual team members to practice engaging in stressful conversations while maintaining the customer service focus previously articulated and in which they are trained.

Facilitating Scenario Discussions

It is not a revelation to note that emotions run high when a library faces a challenge. These emotions are also present as your team runs scenarios, although these are probably more muted. For scenarios to provide the growth and bonding intended, leaders need to guide the resulting conversations as effective strategies develop and acknowledge the team's emotions while supporting individuals in harnessing those emotions to use them constructively. Open, accepting, honest, and trusting sharing among team members is a must at this time. These bonds help your team members avoid internal misunderstandings and accumulating resentment, feelings of isolation, and unacknowledged emotions that can become a catalyst for strife, further complicating an already complex situation. The following exploration of these strategies sheds some light on this.

Words Are Important

Language needs to be used intentionally and chosen with care. The words that first come to mind are probably not the ones that you should use in a sensitive interaction. Nobody needs to know what expletives may swim through your mind; what is vital is ensuring that nothing slips out when engaged with an external challenger. That process includes building on previous teamwork, acknowledging where your team is starting emotionally, foreshadowing the process, and anticipating conflict.

Build on Previous Teamwork

At this point in team preparation, you have reviewed and discussed your organization's official policies in depth. Remember to schedule reviews and conversations regularly to keep procedures fresh and to support new team members as they are onboarded.

Acknowledge Where Your Team Is Starting Emotionally

It is time to take the team's understanding of policy and procedures and apply it to authentic situations. As is true throughout this process, each library team's lived experience varies: some team members must prepare for challenges even as they recover from a recent challenge, are facing an immediate challenge, or are preparing for a circumstance that has not yet developed. The guidance applies to each unique situation but requires adaptation by the library leader facilitating the work.

Foreshadow the Process and Purpose of Running Scenarios

This is not the time for a pop quiz. While you may choose to use a scenario that has not been shared in advance, it is important, particularly the first few times through, for team members to know that the scenario will be part of the team meeting. You want to give them time to rehearse individually in anticipation of the activity. This provides an opportunity for emotional responses to be experienced and brought forward with the team.

Anticipate and Understand Conflict

Conflict results from real or perceived threats in three main areas: reputation, relationship, and money/power. This is true for both internal and external conflicts. Identifying the area of concern causing the conflict can aid in its resolution.

One of the most challenging things to do is to work at conflict resolution as an interested party. In this situation, it is vital to maintain your awareness of the outcome that best serves the organization. Outcomes must always be considered when initiating conflict resolution. Generally, these outcomes can be grouped into three types: worst possible outcome, best possible outcome, and most likely outcome. As a leader of the organization, you must strive to address conflict from a neutral place. To reveal frustration over the cause of a concern raised or

Censorship Scenarios to Workshop: What Will You Do When . . . ?

- A parent contacts a public library director about a graphic novel that his nine-year-old checked out from the juvenile section of the library. He is concerned about what he considers content too mature for nine-year-olds. Upon hearing the concern, the director checks the recommended age range and sees that the novel is intended for young adults.
- During a check-in meeting, a team member raises an objection to the handling of a situation involving mental health issues in a picture book in their library's collection. They would like the title removed not only from their collections but also from all the collections in the library system.
- A note demanding that a long list of titles be removed from the library collection is mailed to all members of your library board. The board in turn contacts you to act on the request.
- A parent and young child pass a display of books and promotional materials for an adult program. The child has questions about the images on display. The uncomfortable parent demands that the display be dismantled.

For additional scenario ideas, use this QR code or go to **knowledgequest.aasl.org/soft-censorship-scenarios-what-would-you-do/** to access the AASL's Knowledge Question blog article, "Soft Censorship Scenarios – What Would You Do?"

procedure objected to is to weaken the trust that will be fundamental to establishing a united team, while likely moving the team toward the "worst possible outcome." Should this occur, acknowledge your reaction as unhelpful and strive to proceed with care and compassion. This is demanding and requires as much practice for organizational leaders as it does for team members.

Be in Tune with Your Reaction

Our communication style may be altered when we respond with emotion. Not that showing emotion is to be avoided; it is often quite reasonable to be emotional, but it is important to be aware of how that changes your communication. Team members will respond emotionally and need compassionate support and guidance to manage their reactions and retain the ability to be intentional in their responses. With this reality in mind, we will spend time focusing on supporting the staff's mental and emotional well-being during times of stress.

Facilitating Team Scenario Discussions

Anticipation, preparation, and practice are at the foundation of all our work in developing our library teams to be challenge-ready. Your work in implementing scenario discussions is no different. Here is an analysis of an actual situation as experienced by Val:

Encountering the Fact Checker

Whether it was an unexpected phone call or a cryptic message to return a phone call, the initial conversation with the "fact checker" caught me entirely off guard.

The phone call with an unknown member of my local community was confusing, frustrating, and unsettling. I imagine that it was experienced in much the same way on the other end of the line as well.

The caller shared that they had learned on a local radio show that public schools were encouraging students to engage in unsafe sex and to address any unwanted pregnancy that might result with an abortion. They had heard that materials promoting abortion and casual sex were readily available in the school library. An additional concern was the belief that school libraries did not have any bibles in their collection and it was indeed illegal for them to have bibles at school.

The caller was an older member of the community and did not have direct ties to the school via children or grandchildren. Yet, they were worried by what they had heard on the radio and could not believe that circumstances had changed so much from what they had experienced or assumed about their local public school.

Perhaps due to the age and bit of uncertainty on the part of the caller, and definitely due to my being caught off guard and feeling defensive, our conversation began to reflect heightened emotions. I asked clarifying questions. The caller struggled to respond, having no real specifics for the inquiry except for the sensational "facts" shared by the radio talk show host. At one point, the caller responded to a tersely delivered question with "I guess I'm really not sure. I'm trying to figure it out."

Fortunately, the sincerity of that reply and the vulnerability of the admission of uncertainty got through to me. It allowed me to recognize my defensive emotions and the tension that my blunt questioning was bringing to the exchange. It allowed me to pause, actually think (always important), and find the space and inspiration to suggest that perhaps scheduling a meeting to discuss the concerns would be helpful. This would allow the caller to take some time to identify the specific concerns they would like addressed, and it would allow me to take a breath and recognize that this type of call is exactly what we teach our school's students to do when they have questions and need information. Rather than blindly assuming that the radio talk show host was correct about every public school, including their own, this citizen wanted to learn more.

We scheduled a meeting to be held in the school library. It was at least a few days and perhaps as much as a week after the initial phone conversation. This allowed us both to regroup and prepare. It also allowed me to alert my principal and a district administrator. During those conversations, I learned that the caller had been trying to reach several other members of the school team with similar concerns regarding the content of our science program and other areas of instruction. No other recipient of those requests for conversation and information had responded to the caller.

When the day of our meeting arrived, the caller toured the school library, and we chatted about what had been heard on the radio talk show and the concerns that had resulted. We browsed the religion collection, noting several versions of the bible as well as areas of the collection focusing on health and relationships. We walked through all of the stacks. In the biography collection, the caller recognized a much-loved book, *The Hiding Place* by Corrie Ten Boom. That connection with something familiar resulted in another shift in perspective, and our conversation became much friendlier. Instead of being a tour of defense it was one of discovery.

The caller departed an hour or so after arriving, much relieved, feeling heard and respected. And I too was much relieved, feeling heard and respected *and* having much to consider and learn from regarding my managing of the inquiry from start to finish. I'm happy to have the opportunity to share some of those lessons with you here.

Postmortem for Learning and Empowerment

Looking back, I recognized that my initial reaction to this phone call was to resent being questioned about my program. It made me feel doubted as a professional. In reality, again, the caller was doing exactly what we hope someone with questions will do: they reached out to the professional to ask questions. Everyone in a library community has the right to ask questions and expect answers. This was the point in my career when I realized that the level of intentionality in my work would enable me to explain and share both the overriding mission of my library and how that mission is carried out in daily practice.

That pause and the recognition of heightening emotions were fortunate gifts. Having time and space to regroup, gather our thoughts, and prepare for our conversation benefited both of us. In particular, this experience allowed me to learn that others in my organization were actively avoiding the caller. It allowed me to consider how to present my physical space to the larger community and to plan which aspects of the collection to highlight during our meeting and tour.

The invitation to come to the library immediately sent a message that there was nothing to hide. It also conveyed that we could remain in conversation as we explored the concerns and misconceptions to the fact checker's satisfaction. I will note here that this exchange never reached a point where there was conversation about the request for reconsideration process. While that is absolutely where I feared we were headed, I did not volunteer that information, although I would have shared it had it been requested. My energy and focus were entirely on explanation and satisfaction of the named concerns, and I worked very hard to avoid anticipating trouble and assuming that a challenge was inevitable.

With the extra time to prepare and while discussing the situation with my administrators, I realized that it would be important to convey a business-as-usual experience to the fact checker. Having either of my administrators present would be a signal that we had concerns about the visit and the outcome. Additionally, in my situation, neither of my administrators had any training in addressing inquiries and challenges in the library, and frankly, I had concerns about what they might say during the meeting and tour. The value of planning in advance and communicating with all parties who may be engaged in the process cannot be overstated. I was very fortunate to have the trust of my administrators, both of whom expressed relief that I was equipped to manage the initial meeting without assistance and that I had engaged with the fact checker and taken the pressure of repeated phone call attempts off my colleagues.

Most valuably, the lesson of recognizing our shared concern for the students in our local community and addressing the inquirer's questions and concerns with respect, dedicated time, and attention, as well as courtesy, has guided my practice from that point on. Yes, I still have a moment of annoyance if I feel my professional judgment is being questioned, but being intentional about hearing what is actually being said helps that moment pass. Working to understand the perspective of community members who know very little about libraries is critical. We cannot expect everyone to fully understand our mission and operations. We must welcome the opportunity to share and teach.

Shift to Practical Application for Your Team

Building off your insights based on the breakdown of the "fact checker" story, plan to support your team as they practice using your chosen scenarios and reflect on that experience. Guide them through prep work, a team discussion, and a postmortem review.

Prep Work

- Plan to give prompts and reminders to team members about the content of your library organization's policies and procedures. This helps keep the discussion grounded.
- Review the scenario you will be introducing in order to anticipate the potential flow of team members' actions/responses, both desired and problematic ones.
- Anticipate where your team may get stuck in the process or become more reactive than proactive.
- Determine who is participating in the scenario; depending on the team's size, you will have active participants as well as observers, and both are important to the experience.

Facilitating the Team Scenario Discussion

- Lead a "pre-mortem," discussing the roles that each team member anticipates taking.
- Identify and discuss potential pitfalls.
- Review your team's response flowchart for the discussion.
- Potentially assign roles for each individual to assume and practice, rotating roles.

Lead a Postmortem Review of the Discussion

- Provide time for team members to individually reflect on their experiences.
- Identify insights, pitfalls, unanticipated feelings, ideas, and outcomes.
- Provide an opportunity for each team member to share, either directly or privately with you, their insights, emotions, questions, and frustrations.

- Lead a team discussion, gathering ideas for better supporting each other and clarifying your response to any questions regarding the content of the library's policies and procedures (including the possible need for updates).

Carrying Training Outcomes into the Future

You have now designed a structure for guiding and training your team. Regularly infusing the training with content focused on having and maintaining a challenge-ready team allows you to onboard new team members, update policies, and review and hone the skills of all team members. Your training and response structure also provides a framework for debriefing and course-correcting when actual inquiries or challenges arise. This is evergreen training material that will preserve both team relationships and the integrity of the library as an instrument of intellectual freedom.

Use this QR code or go to **alaeditions.org/webextras** to access the Facilitating Discussion Checklist, a downloadable and editable version of the lists on pages 51–52.

CHRONICLE YOUR JOURNEY!

Which aspects of practicing and rehearsing scenarios will be most challenging, and how can they be addressed?

_____

_____

Carving out time during professional development and regular team meetings?

_____

_____

_____

_____

Grouping team members while in the process of team- and trust-building?

_____
_____
_____
_____
_____

Staying in tune to individual team members' reactions to what can be difficult work?

_____
_____
_____
_____
_____

PART III

WORDS TAKE FLIGHT
Systematizing the Challenge Readiness Plan

Part III of our book leads you through creating systems for maintaining and sharing your action plan. In the chapters that follow, we'll evaluate the current messaging about addressing book challenges, identifying gaps, leveraging opportunities to dispel misinformation, and creating systematic, proactive messaging to address questions that are asked repeatedly. Finally, we will investigate several types of intellectual freedom challenges and how a challenge-ready team might respond to them.

In any organization, turnover is likely to occur, so there will be new hires onboarded, requiring training to address any knowledge gaps. How should you proceed? What should you share? How should you deliver information? How do you teach new staff to navigate conversations? There is much to consider. These questions will be addressed, along with ideas on how to prepare a plan for communicating with stakeholders at all levels.

The importance of clear, concise, and intentional communication is embedded in all intellectual freedom work. Thorough attention to systematic, purposeful communications can result in greater cohesion and clarity for the entire organization.

CHAPTER 7

Systems for Ongoing Readiness and Capacity-Building

Clear is kind. Unclear is unkind.
—BRENÉ BROWN

Systematic, purposeful communication can make a difference in building transparency and trust in the communities you serve and in building capacity in anyone charged with delivering information about policies, procedures, and processes. Communication is an exchange of information, so it is imperative to contemplate both the delivery and reception of the communication. Proactive preparation can help teams to identify what details to share, select the best way to convey them to others, and determine how to navigate the resulting conversations.

As librarians, "we uphold the principles of intellectual freedom and resist all efforts to censor library resources."[1] This is one of several core values that guide our profession. As a guiding principle, it can reduce the anxiety and stress of employees, as well as build relationships and trust between colleagues and leaders and make a difference in how a team handles each situation.

Developing Systems for Onboarding and Maintenance

Every library institution typically maintains a great deal of information regarding its processes and procedures. But oftentimes, the knowledge of these processes and procedures is inside the head of an individual rather than part of the institution. A snag can occur when an individual leaves the institution, creating a void of information for the remaining workers or anyone new who comes in. The reconsideration of library materials is an important process which demands clear, concise, and above all, documented procedures that are explicit for employees to reference should clarity be needed. You should prepare to create documents and systems that will maintain your action plan regardless of team members' turnover.

Assessing Ongoing Team Needs

Determining the current and future needs of the team is the first step. Look at each individual on your team and make a list, sorting members into the following categories:
- New-to-profession hires
- New hires to your organization but not new to librarianship
- Returning staff to your organization

The categories above allow you to differentiate to meet the learning needs of your team; the depth of communication training will also vary based on these categories. Returning staff may need to hear updates and a refresher on procedures but may not require the same intensity of learning as those in the other two categories. Experienced new hires will require procedural training specific to your organization, while new-to-profession hires will require guidance in learning about policies, communication, processes, and procedures. Regardless of the category, breaking down what learning is needed for different team members is an important task for a leader to consider.

Ongoing Training and Onboarding

Libraries have different natural refresher points where action plan updates might take place. For school and academic libraries, this will likely be at the end of summer or the beginning of fall when teachers and students return to school. For public libraries, this is likely more variable: the start of the calendar year is a logical choice, but you may also aim for action plan refreshers in the fall, after summer reading programs have wrapped or at other times that make sense for your organization's hiring cycles. For any organization, a large turnover of staff will require training regardless of the time of year. In addition, any major updates to the library's selection and reconsideration policies and procedures would warrant a staff update.

Beyond annual all-staff updates, be prepared to differentiate professional training for the various categories of staff you've identified. Your newest staff will need support and ongoing training on all kinds of topics throughout at least their first year. Think about how elements of your selection criteria, policies, and action plan can be incorporated into new staff trainings in digestible chunks. When you do this, be sure to connect the content back to the bigger picture of your library's overall plan and policies. Your staff are likely not thinking about the organization and action plan as holistically as you are; help them comprehend the bigger picture by frequently referencing the action plan. Graphic organizers such as concept maps, flowcharts, and Venn diagrams can make your vision visible and comprehensible for your adult learners.

Finally, think about how to utilize your staff to train and support each other's journey toward challenge preparedness. This may look like a train-the-trainer model, where a core group of staff members become the go-to people for questions about intellectual freedom. Alternatively, you may assign "buddies" so team members can learn together. Their different backgrounds and work experiences will enrich and deepen their learning as they help each other consider the work from various perspectives. Buddies can also provide moral support to each other in the case of a difficult challenge.

Developing Systems for Consistent Communication

When you paint a clear picture of your expectations, others within your organization will internalize them, convey the processes clearly to both colleagues and patrons, and be a strong cog in your organizational system. The information you share should encompass any anticipated need. For example, helping staff understand what to say when they don't have a ready answer is an important conversation to have in advance.

Clear Expectations for Communication

Employees may not realize the potential impact of their response to patron inquiries. In the current climate, many documented cases have gone viral that illustrate a conversation gone awry. In an employee handbook, consider including guiding documents showing examples of actions and body language that may either facilitate open communications or escalate communications in a negative direction; this facilitates a clarity that is explicit and easily put into practice. Review these actions as a team and discuss how each action impacts the conversation; this can reduce stress and proactively prepare your team for situations they may face. Table 7.1 details actions that can make users feel heard and understood, and those that can further frustrate a tense user.

TABLE 7.1

Actions that facilitate or escalate communications

ACTIONS THAT FACILITATE OPEN COMMUNICATIONS	ACTIONS THAT CAN ESCALATE CHARGED COMMUNICATIONS
Ask for time.	Use an adversarial tone.
Use open and non-confrontational body language (hands to sides, neutral face).	Take a defensive stance (arms crossed or on hips, stern face).
Just listen if you're not sure what to say.	Talk just to fill space.
If you must send an e-mail, take time before sending and have colleagues review it first.	Send an e-mail when you're in an emotional state.
Utilize face-to-face or phone conversations to communicate clearly with tone and body language.	Ignore the inquirer's concern or avoid any follow-up.
Take the opportunity for gentle education.	Speak in a condescending tone or with lots of jargon.

Navigating Conversations as a Coach

While actions and body language can play an important role in communication, crafting your message while keeping the other person's feelings and opinions in mind is equally important. There should be no assumptions regarding the inquirer's viewpoint or motives; seeking to understand their concern is the priority. Moreover, it is human nature to want to show empathy or compassion when engaging with questions about books, but this is a situation where simply agreeing with the inquirer could create additional issues for your institution. Instead, teaching employees to reiterate concerns, offer alternative options for readers, and share reminders about the mission of libraries will help to build the inquirer's understanding of your organization's purpose while still acknowledging the specific needs around their concern.

As a leader, it is imperative that you put yourself in the role of a coach rather than a problem-solver as you plan to teach these skills. Coaching uses guiding questions to help trainees reflect and build connections on their own. It would be so easy to swoop in, fix the issue, and tell employees what to say. But while this may fix the problem, it does not build capacity within your team. Leaders cannot always be present or may not be available to navigate the conversation in a library, so a priority goal should be to train your employees. The phrases in table 7.2 offer examples of communications that can facilitate or escalate a conversation.

TABLE 7.2

Phrases that facilitate or escalate communications

PHRASES THAT FACILITATE OPEN COMMUNICATIONS	PHRASES THAT CAN ESCALATE CHARGED COMMUNICATIONS
✓ "Tell me more about. . ."	⊘ "It doesn't make sense to. . ."
✓ "Can you clarify for me. . . ?"	⊘ "Are you kidding me?!"
✓ "Let me make sure I've got everything. . ."	⊘ "I don't think you understand. . ."
✓ "Did I miss anything?"	⊘ "Absolutely not."
✓ "Please tell me what happened."	⊘ "I can't make changes for you/your student."
✓ "I'm glad that you are engaging with <insert name's> reading."	⊘ "This isn't your private library."
✓ "Some ways I address this situation are. . ."	⊘ "That's not possible."
✓ "Here are some ways that I can support meeting the needs of your reader. . ."	⊘ "I don't have time for this."
✓ "I'm glad to have this opportunity to work together to find a good solution."	⊘ "You should understand. . ."
✓ "Thank you for taking the time to raise this concern."	⊘ "It is your job to monitor what your reader checks out."
✓ "I'd like to gather some resources for us. Can we schedule a time to reconnect?"	⊘ "I can't get to this right now. This will need to wait."

After you review the phrases above, ask the following questions of your employees:
- How did you feel saying what you did? What caused you to feel that way?
- How could you continue to increase your comfort with tense conversations?
- What do you think went well?
- If you could have a do-over, what would you do differently?
- What is something you wish you would have said but didn't?

"Practice makes perfect" applies to this exercise; the more a leader engages employees in rehearsal and reflection, the better employees will become at having conversations. In addition, the more you as the leader practice using coaching questions and statements, the more natural it will feel to let your staff draw their own conclusions. This will take patience and forethought, so before going into a conversation, write down a coaching prompt you would like to try. Here are some sample coaching sentence frames:
- What would happen if you tried...?
- What decisions made that interaction successful?
- When you were speaking, I observed...
- It sounds like...

Sharing Research to Build Morale and Capacity

Library professionals are living in unprecedented, historic times; as authors and fellow professionals, we recognize the emotional and stressful toll that intellectual freedom conversations on the front line can have on a person's well-being. Sharing research which supports the work library professionals do is information that leaders can pass along to their employees to build confidence, instill hope, and reduce stress.

In a March 2022 ALA press release, findings from Hart Research Associates and North Star Opinion Research (completed on behalf of ALA) among 1,000 voters and 472 parents of students attending public schools yielded the following data:[2]
- Large majorities of voters (71 percent) oppose efforts to have books removed.
- Most voters and parents hold librarians in high regard *and* have confidence in their libraries to make good decisions about collection purchases.
- Most voters and parents agree that libraries in their communities do a good job offering a variety of viewpoints via the books and resources in their collections.

When we ban or restrict access to books, we deprive patrons of the opportunity to see themselves reflected in stories, fully engage in their learning, and grapple with the complexity of the real world in which they live and which they must navigate.[3] Access is a core library principle that we need to remember and circle back to whenever we face and work through book challenges. Reviewing research and sharing new findings with employees will provide a beacon of hope during very trying times and will center the work done on behalf of the readers who want to see the representation of diverse viewpoints and cultures on our shelves.

CHRONICLE YOUR JOURNEY!

Categorize your employees into the three categories listed earlier in this chapter. How will the number of employees listed in each category impact how you plan your next training?

_____

_____

_____

Review your current written procedures for inquiries regarding book challenges and reconsiderations. Make a list of what is missing and what needs to be added.

_____

_____

_____

After reading this chapter, what ideas, questions, or action steps do you want to use to inform your work as you consider how to build team capacity?

_____

_____

_____

NOTES

1. American Library Association, "Core Values of Librarianship," last modified January 2019, www.ala.org/advocacy/advocacy/intfreedom/corevalues.
2. American Library Association, "Voters Oppose Book Bans in Libraries," www.ala.org/advocacy/voters-oppose-book-bans-libraries.
3. American Library Association, "Empowered by Reading: The Benefits of Giving Youth Access to a Wide Variety of Reading Materials," Unite Against Book Bans, https://uniteagainstbookbans.org/wp-content/uploads/2022/09/Empowered-by-Reading-final.pdf.

CHAPTER 8

Planning for Clear Communication with All Stakeholders

The most important thing in communication is hearing what isn't said.
—PETER DRUCKER

It is important for library leaders to reflect on any previous censorship experiences and glean takeaways for improvement. Book challenge interactions can be difficult to navigate, but the adversity we undergo has the potential to instruct us, reveal gaps in our procedures, and help us to refine our library processes. It is critical to understand and consider the *probletunity*—problem + opportunity—and allow it to be a catalyst for our organizations to continuously improve.

Harnessing multiple perspectives ensures that you don't overlook any potential entry points for improvement. Every stakeholder's input offers the chance to evaluate their unique information needs and address these in a differentiated manner. Effective leaders examine stakeholder input with humility and curiosity, and then use it to move forward. Your stakeholder information-gathering will inevitably be a study in human behavior with the goal of pinpointing current information needs, creating the documents and guidance to fill the gaps, and deploying the communications to the appropriate stakeholders.

Gathering Stakeholder Needs

As leaders, we work with a variety of people and engage with many stakeholders—district- or management-level library leaders, our own library teams, and administrators, to name a few—and each group provides a unique and important perspective. Many of us will have similar experiences, but it is in the nuances of our many personal interactions that we find opportunities to glean new ways to address issues, questions, and misinformation. Below are some suggested groups and reflective questions to consider in order to ensure that your action plan is communicated to the right stakeholders.

District- and Management-Level Leaders

As the head of your leadership team, consider asking the following questions of anyone who is under your immediate supervision or any positions you support. Those individuals will also want to take this to their team members, such as assistants, circulation desk staff, and other librarians they supervise, if applicable.

Individuals you may collaborate with should be included too.
- What questions from stakeholders do you keep addressing via phone or e-mail?
- What do you repeatedly see being asked on social media?
- What questions or misconceptions regarding book challenges do you have to address repeatedly?
- What stakeholder groups keep asking questions?

Whether it is librarians, principals, parents, library boards, or community members who ask the questions, your compiled responses could indicate a potential need for clear communication. You cannot know the needs of each and every stakeholder, but this information-seeking will help you to fill any knowledge gaps, so you might not have to answer those same questions in the future.

The Affinity Exercise: A Process Improvement Tool

One process improvement tool that enables many participants to provide feedback is called an "affinity exercise." In this exercise, the leader shares one question, and participants jot down one answer to the question per sticky note. The participants jot down as many answers as possible to the question. Once all the participants are done answering the individual question, all their answers are shared as a group and compiled into categories. The categories are labeled so that the leader can understand the overarching answer; all the sticky note suggestions are reviewed so that the readers can understand how this category was labeled. The total number of sticky-note examples you get will depend on the number of participants. There will be outlier questions, but the hope is you will get a good grasp of questions that continually rise to the top. Below is an example using the following question: *What questions do you have about reconsideration processes?*

Affinity exercise example

Communication	Training Needs	Library-Related Processes
Questions about policy	What should I say if I get an e-mail about a book?	What should I do if I'm unsure about book placement?
How are books selected?	My administrator is asking about book challenge processes.	How often do librarians get trained?
How do you determine where a book is placed?		Is it okay to share our selection policy?

Sample Toolkits for Navigating the Landscape

In this current censorship climate, there are many organizations, and grassroots groups that have produced and shared great toolkits to build understanding and awareness about intellectual freedom. These toolkits offer great talking points that can serve as mentor text as you launch into creating resources for your organization. Here are a few toolkits to consider:

- **American Library Association:** www.ala.org/advocacy/bbooks
- **Unite Against Book Bans:** https://uniteagainstbookbans.org/
- **National Coalition Against Censorship:** https://ncac.org/resource/educator-handbook
- **PEN America:** https://pen.org/issue/book-bans/
- **Texas #FReadom Fighters:** www.txfreadomfighters.us/

The Library Team

Next turn to your librarian team and ask them the following questions:
- What do you wish parents, library users, and community members understood about the processes and procedures for materials selection?
- What do administrators and parents know about how you select books?
- What questions are continually asked when a community member reaches out to you regarding books?
- What questions do you feel have not been addressed in policy and procedure training that you feel are needed?

You should use a data-gathering method that allows everyone to participate and share while keeping their responses brief. Time is of the essence, and having to read over long-form answers could be a barrier to their use. For example, you may add these kinds of questions to exit slip surveys at the end of professional development sessions or as a "sponge activity," a connector to facilitate engagement as folks flow in at the start of meetings. Whether you use tech or analog tools, data gathered regularly will provide important input for adjusting your approach.

Administrators and Board Members

No administrator or board member, whether in the city or school district, wants to be caught off guard and put a foot wrong in a tense situation. They may have information needs of their own that they don't express, but as library leaders, we must be cognizant of their time constraints and schedules. A survey link might be the easiest, simplest, most direct, and efficient way to capture their feedback. You can populate the resulting answers to assess their understanding and offer opportunities for open-ended responses to consider additional needs. Here are some questions to pose:
- Do you understand the policies and procedures regarding book reconsiderations?
- Do you have a plan in place should a library user or community member contact you to ask questions regarding a book challenge?
- Have you met with your librarian to discuss a communication plan on how to handle any questions about books?
- What are some action steps library leaders can take to help you better understand library processes?
- What support do you need in navigating conversations with community members who are raising concerns?

Once all the responses have been received, you can review the answers to each question. Assess the group as a whole on their understanding of procedures and policies. Read over the open-ended questions and look for patterns in order to spot potential needs. Common needs may arise, and this is where your communication opportunities lie. Leverage what you learn in order to determine the next steps.

Working with Individuals

The examples above are focused on groups, but it's also important to remember that you might field questions from individuals within your organization or community. Each of those individual engagements is just as important and can also shed insight on your overall communication plan. You should try to learn from conversations what pieces of information might address misunderstandings before they cause conflict. Consider the following as you work with each individual:
- Affirm the needs of the person you are speaking to.
- Listen with an open mind and acknowledge the person's needs.
- Ask clarifying questions to ensure that you fully understand the issue or concern.
- There will be times when you won't have the answer to a question. Tell the person that you want to provide accurate information, and offer to reach out to them once you have the information.
- If you are in a situation that is emotionally charged, share reminders about being respectful; it's also okay to excuse yourself in order to get additional support.

A Communication Plan for All Stakeholders

The exercises above should shed light on information gaps and uncover needs for you to address as a system. Take the time to be thoughtful and strategic about how you will proceed. Your communication plan should take into consideration the needs and priorities of your stakeholder groups, as well as the best ways to reach them.

Core Documents

Your updated policies and procedures and the action plan you created are your foundational documents. Who needs access to these in full? The librarians you work with are an obvious answer, but consider who else will be impacted should a challenge occur.
- *Governing board:* They likely will have approved the policies, but they should also have access to the procedures and departmental documents that will guide your work. Use your judgment and knowledge of your institution to determine how much information your board needs.
- *Non-library administrators:* Depending on your library type, you may interact with administrators who are not directly serving libraries. Consider which of these individuals need access to your plans. For example, many school library programs exist within district Teaching and Learning departments; the leaders in these departments should have access to core documents.

- *Support staff:* Assistants, aides, and other nonprofessional staff should know where to access your core documents and be aware of their role in the action plan.
- *Communications Department:* If your organization has a dedicated Communications Department, make sure they know where your documents can be accessed. In your action plan, you probably identified a role for them, and they will need to know where they fit.
- *Legal Department:* An institution's legal counsel may have been part of the policy update or creation process. Let them know where they can find the documentation that supports the policies.

While access to full documents is important, creating summary materials for your team and organization can also be very helpful. At Madison, we have a two-sided document that highlights the major takeaways of our selection criteria and process for our library team to keep on hand while selecting materials for purchase. A QR code and shortened URL grace the upper corner of it for access to the full documents. This kind of chart can also serve as a quick reference for administrators, support staff, and other employees in your organization who may benefit from an abbreviated version of your core documents.

Public-Facing Documents

Your organization's board policies should already be posted for public access. You may also want to include information on the selection and reconsideration process for public view. A great way to present this information is an FAQ (frequently asked questions) document. Consider the following items as a starting point in an FAQ, and make it more applicable to your community by utilizing the stakeholder questions you have collected.
- What is the overall purpose of your library collection?
- How are materials selected for your library?
- How do you decide which materials go in which area of the library and at which level of the collection?
- Where do the funds to purchase library materials come from?
- What should I do if I have a question about an item in your library?

Infographics can present information in a readily digestible format, using color, shape, and numbers to paint a picture for the viewer. Circulation statistics, the makeup of your collection (i.e., fiction versus nonfiction and print versus digital), and brief snippets of your policy can make good infographic elements. Infographics might also consist of components of an annual report; you can maximize efficiency by keeping track of which infographic items could make useful points in your report and vice versa.

When considering which formats to use for your various audiences, keep in mind how they will use the information. For those who need to internalize and implement the documents, include details and examples, but organize these in a manner that quickly demonstrates the overall structure of the plan. For library users, who are potentially your library champions, keep the information brief and impactful so it is memorable and easy to share with others.

Once your documents are ready, go back to the people who provided the feedback and have them look over and read anything new you have created. Let them know that their feedback was a catalyst for initiating the updates you made. Ask them if your new information speaks to the needs they have. Once everything has been reviewed, determine where you want to post the new information and share it widely with the stakeholders who will be impacted or who need the support.

Delivery of Information to Stakeholders

While you probably don't have the authority to decide where board policy is posted, you can control where to place your departmental documents. Like a grocery store merchandiser, think about where your stakeholders will already be looking and then place the relevant information there. Do you maintain a website or folder of information for your library staff? Put your core documents there. Do you have a public-facing library website? Post your FAQ there, perhaps in an *About Us* section. You may also want to print your FAQ and have it handy at the circulation desk, particularly if you serve an aging community; they may prefer paper over electronic access.

Communication as Advocacy

Clear, systematic communication has so many benefits: it strengthens your unified team response, alleviates team members' anxiety, and ultimately makes the implementation of the challenge-ready action plan possible. Communication is also the bedrock of advocacy and coalition-building. Giving stakeholders a window into your values, priorities, and processes provides an opportunity for them to step up as partners and advocates for your library. Whether these partners are libraries, families, professional organizations, or community leaders, their ability to speak on your behalf has the potential to make a huge difference during a tense challenge. Their voices can validate your library's crucial role in the community because they can speak with more distance and objectivity than anyone in your organization can. Work toward building a coalition early and maintain it even in calmer times. Leverage your team's connections in the community to spread a wider net—you may discover advocates in unexpected places—and use your newly built communication documents to send a strong and clear message.

The author and inspirational speaker Simon Sinek once said, "No one knows everything. But together, we know a whole lot." This is even more applicable in these very challenging times. The sheer volume of challenges has provided many library leaders with an opportunity to learn much and refine their communication processes very quickly. Lean on your professional organizations and network with colleagues to share your ideas and best practices. Never forget that we are stronger together!

CHRONICLE YOUR JOURNEY!

Consider all the stakeholder groups you serve. What opportunities exist to strengthen these groups' understanding of library processes when it comes to the reconsideration process?

_____
_____
_____
_____
_____
_____
_____

What are the topics of communication regarding intellectual freedom that need to be documented and/or reviewed?

_____
_____
_____
_____
_____
_____
_____

Consider any past communications or interactions where stakeholders inquired about processes. Did those inquiries focus on anything specific?

_____
_____
_____
_____
_____
_____

Are there any written policies or procedures that could be turned into infographics to build understanding?

_____

_____

_____

_____

_____

Make a list of stakeholders you'd like to work with in order to gauge their understanding of policies and procedures.

_____

_____

_____

_____

_____

CHAPTER 9

Applying Your Plan to Various Scenarios

We all have experienced various inquiries and challenges that came from different sources and were resolved in different ways. We have seen our colleagues in libraries of all types do the same thing. Through them we have gained insights and learned lessons that inform the resources we have provided to guide you in preparing for similar experiences. Each challenge to intellectual freedom contains its own nuances that can ignite anxieties and uncertainties. But whether the challenge comes from inside the building, from a community-led action, or from an out-of-state organization, many of the same approaches will support you in any of those situations.

The Call Came from Inside the Building

While many challenges arise from the patrons and families we serve, some questions come from within our own organizations. We observed one such challenge related to a book that was being used widely in middle school social studies instruction. The district Department of Curriculum and Instruction had purchased multiple copies of this title for use in classrooms before deciding that the book should have been accompanied by guidance for teachers about teaching about race and racism. They pulled back the book temporarily, seeking to ensure that educators did not unintentionally cause harm to students and families.

When one school administrator received the directive to pull back instructional copies of the book, he also requested that the school librarian pull back her library copies of the title. The librarian knew that the library's selection and reconsideration guidelines differed from those for instructional materials, so she told her administrator that she would not be removing the books from her library collection. He took issue with her refusal, not understanding the distinction between an instructional material taught to all students in the classroom and a library book available for students to freely choose.

At this point the librarian reached out to her district leaders, who were able to confirm that the library copies would need to stay in the collection unless a formal challenge was filed. The administrator relented, but his relationship with the librarian in his school was damaged.

In another scenario, a school district administrator became concerned at the increasing number of book challenges in neighboring communities. He found the list of books being reconsidered in a nearby district and, fearing conflict in his own district, pulled copies of the books from the high school libraries to restrict access while deciding what to do. The district library coordinator was asked to review the books, although no request for reconsideration had been completed by the administrator or anyone else. In one incredibly high-level administrative restriction, the mayor of Fort Worth, Texas, ordered the city's public library to remove the "Pride Challenge" badge as an option in the mayor's summer reading program.[1] It is helpful to be aware that intellectual freedom challenges can come from any source, including your own leaders.

Applying a Team Preparedness Approach

Strong policy is an important first step in approaching situations where challenges arise from the leadership within your organization. However, in both of the scenarios just described, there were policies in place that were either not known or ignored by the administration. During the recent uptick in book challenges, it has not been uncommon for administrators, library boards, and school boards to ignore their organization's own policies and procedures in fear-based, knee-jerk reactions.

Our recommendation is that libraries engage in proactive coalition-building and educating within their own institutions. While it is essential that a library have partnerships with other library types and intellectual freedom organizations, understanding must be built on your home turf first. Clear, widely known policies and procedures can prevent misunderstandings between librarians seeking to protect their users' right to read and well-meaning leaders who are juggling multiple priorities, from funding to public relations.

It is especially important that all parties in your organization know your selection policy and not only your reconsideration policy. Having a detailed selection policy that all parties know well is one of the strongest defenses against threats to intellectual freedom. It ensures that selectors of library materials know why they have selected the materials they have and can provide strong evidence when addressing a question. It also allows a librarian to regularly review the contents of the collection against a set of criteria. For example, a public library may reference its selection policy when determining where to place a book: in the juvenile, young adult, or adult section. A school librarian can use the criteria and professional reviews when deciding whether the age range the library serves is the intended audience for a book. The selection policy should also stipulate that the library collection will be diverse and representative of your library users, which can help to stave off self-censorship by library staff. Do not underestimate the defining power of a clear and well-known selection policy.

Three-Ring Media Circus

Recently, media attention has been a tool for those who seek to restrict access to books in libraries. At one district's school board meeting, parents and community members took turns reading aloud passages from young adult novels that were taken out of context, with intention to shock the audience and put the school board in an uncomfortable position. The press reported on this, as well as name-calling and shouting from meeting attendees. Ultimately, the books in question, all covering LGBTQ+ topics, were removed from school libraries in the district.

Applying a Team Preparedness Approach

This level of public attention and scrutiny feels very different from a one-on-one conversation with a library user. However, in some ways the approach will look the same in both situations. Be prepared to manage your emotions and stick to established scripts, whether you're addressing a single questioner or a boardroom full of people and press. This is an excellent time to engage a preestablished press point person who is equipped to speak confidently under the stress of the public eye. In addition, prepare your board in advance for potentially contentious meetings. In an article for *Library Journal*, EveryLibrary founder John Chrastka recommends that school boards review not just the policies related to library materials, but also their meeting protocols in order to maintain orderly proceedings.[2] While you cannot control the press or your board members, you can prepare yourself and your team as thoroughly as possible—and reflect on unforeseen circumstances so as to strengthen your approach next time.

Do I Know You?

Ideally, families or library patrons approach their community librarians to inquire about a book or program. At times, as discussed previously, the inquiry comes from within the organization itself. Unfortunately, sometimes a challenge arises from someone completely disconnected from your library, often politically motivated groups. It is becoming more common for social media and websites to recommend books for removal, largely targeting books with LGBTQ+ and antiracist themes. These sites spur people on to demand that books be removed from their local libraries; moreover, the sites often provide form letters or language that result in immediate formal reconsiderations and skip opportunities for conversation and bridge-building.

One such case took place in the small town of Mount Horeb, Wisconsin, in 2015. Teachers in the elementary school shared plans to read aloud *I Am Jazz*, a picture-book autobiography of the transgendered media personality Jazz Jennings, in support of a transgendered girl at their school. Word of this plan reached a Florida organization called the Liberty Counsel, which sent a letter to the school board threatening a lawsuit.

In response, the board penned a policy explicitly protecting transgendered students in their district. The high school's Sexuality and Gender Alliance read aloud *I Am Jazz* to an audience of 200. A reading at the Mount Horeb Public Library to a crowd of more than 600 followed later that night.[3]

Applying a Team Preparedness Approach

This exceptional example illustrates the power of community libraries coming together. While the elementary school paused before reading *I Am Jazz*, the high school and public library felt positioned to take a chance and conduct readings. What a powerful communication of support this was for transgendered individuals in the city, as well as for the librarians and educators of the Mount Horeb school district. The Public Library Association's president, Melanie Huggins, asserts that when school libraries in a community are under fire, that is the moment for public libraries to partner with them to extend support.[4] It is never too late to connect with other libraries in your area to coordinate efforts and develop a partnership. Even the opportunity to commiserate and provide moral support to one another is worth the time it takes to connect.

This scenario also reminds us that library policy can and should specify who can submit a reconsideration request. The needs of our library users are our priority. Individuals from outside our communities must not be allowed to restrict access to materials for our students, families, and neighbors.

Reflecting and Adjusting—Again and Again

Whether or not you ever face a challenge like the examples above, take time to reflect on what they can teach you and your team about challenge readiness. Reflecting on your action plan and adjusting to meet new circumstances or to support your team better is a never-ending process. Your policies and procedures can never be fully completed or perfected when the state of your organization, community, and world is ever evolving. The beauty of our work is that it spurs us to continuously grow and change with the needs of our users. Give yourself time also to dwell on your growth and successes. Breathe, congratulate yourself and your team, and gear up to reflect and adjust once more.

CHRONICLE YOUR JOURNEY!

What types of scenarios do you feel your team is best equipped to respond to confidently?

_____
_____
_____
_____

What strengths and structures are in place to support this?

_____
_____
_____
_____

What conditions or structures need to be revised or created?

_____
_____
_____
_____

After reading this chapter, what ideas, questions, or action steps do you want to use to inform your work as you consider different challenges you might encounter with your team?

_____
_____
_____
_____

NOTES

1. Adriana De Alba, "Pride Challenge Removed from Fort Worth Mayor's Summer Reading Challenge after Complaints," WFAA, May 26, 2023, www.wfaa.com/article/news/local/pride-challenge-removed-fort-worth-mayors-summer-reading-challenge-complaints/287-70facef4-855f-4d46-99c2-d050f3e768da.
2. Amy Rea, "Public Libraries Face Escalating Book Challenges," *Library Journal*, March 14, 2022, www.libraryjournal.com/story/Public-Libraries-Face-Escalating-Book-Challenges.
3. American Booksellers Association, "Mount Horeb Says 'No' to Censorship," December 16, 2016, www.bookweb.org/news/mount-horeb-says-%E2%80%9Cno%E2%80%9D-censorship.
4. Rea, "Public Libraries."

CONCLUSION
Prepared and Empowered to Defend

The prevalence of challenges to intellectual freedom that we are currently experiencing demands our urgent attention. Library teams that are prepared to respond in an organized and cohesive manner will be more effective in communicating within their organization and community. That is the work that has been undertaken in this book.

As you have considered and planned to take your team through the process of reviewing and updating foundational documents, you have begun the work of expanding your team's capacity to respond to questions in a uniform and confident manner. This work alone strengthens your organization.

Library staff guided by a response team acting on a carefully crafted action plan are better able to carefully consider and respond openly to questions regarding matters of intellectual freedom. They have trained and practiced in order to seek understanding, act supportively, and validate their community members' right to know as highly as they do their right to read.

Communication must be clear and consistent for both internal and external stakeholders. Addressing this need and designing intentional messaging for every diverse audience is culminating work in preparing your library team to handle challenges as efficiently and effectively as possible.

As your library dives into this work, each member of your organization will play a vital role. Together you will create solid foundational documents and identify responders to whom team members can direct inquiries and who are well practiced in addressing those inquiries in a professional and knowledgeable manner. Unified by a board, director, and managers who have implemented a system for clarity in communication, your library organization will benefit from the support of your community, among whom you and your team are well known and connected. This is our hope for you, your team, and your library.

Thank you for taking on this work. Although it is daunting, it has immeasurable value. Do not reinvent the wheel and do not travel this road alone.

APPENDIX
Team-Building Resources

Trainings

Crisis Prevention Institute (crisisprevention.com) offers multiple trainings on how to identify and interpret crisis behaviors and de-escalate heightened situations. Organizations can pay for training or have their individuals become trainers.

Mediate University (mediateuniversity.com) offers training in conflict mediation. The basic forty-hour mediation training is a worthwhile investment when training managers and response team members.

National Association for Community Mediation (nafcm.org) offers training and toolkits for "Cultivating Allies," "Navigating Cultural Differences," and "Legislative Toolkit." A membership fee is required to access the toolkit content.

Thinking Collaborative's (thinkingcollaborative.com) Adaptive Schools training provides meeting facilitation skills and protocols for a fee. Many of their protocols are available for free on their website.

Publications

Conflict Management for Managers: Resolving Workplace, Client, and Policy Disputes, by Susan S. Raines.
Beginning with conflict styles, this resource explores all aspects of workplace conflict in depth. The level of detail provides a depth of coverage that allows readers to recognize similar circumstances and situations in their own organization.

The Conflict Pivot: Turning Conflict into Peace of Mind, by Tammy Lenski.
Presenting three concrete strategies for reframing and resetting contentious situations, this book provides a lens into the behaviors that contribute to conflict and how they can be addressed.

Crucial Conversations: Tools for Talking When Stakes Are High, by Kerry Patterson et al.
Addressing conflict takes courage. One of the most daunting aspects of taking action is knowing what to say while fearing to make the conflict worse. *Crucial Conversations* provides guidance for broaching tense topics and repairing the damage caused by conversational errors.

Mastering Civility: A Manifesto for the Workplace, by Christine Porath.
All workplace challenges are more difficult if there is a culture of incivility. Organizations benefit in productivity and output when their employees have respectful relationships. This resource aids in identifying and addressing incivility among coworkers and beyond.

Radical Candor: Be a Kick-Ass Boss without Losing Your Humanity, by Kim Scott.
This book is the business industry standard for communicating clearly and directly, and addressing internal problems while maintaining respectful and supportive relationships.

Turn Enemies into Allies: The Art of Peace in the Workplace, by Judy Ringer.
This is an excellent resource for resetting relationships through perspective-taking and acknowledging the role that individuals play in contributing to ongoing disputes.

ALA Resource

ALA Ecosystem Initiative – One Voice Toolkit (www.ala.org/advocacy/ala-ecosystem-initiative). The One Voice toolkit helps library organizations assess and extend the strength of their ecosystems, and identify and pursue priorities for advocacy and legislation. While written for ecosystems at the state level, the framework can be applied to the library ecosystem at any level and can include a wide range of library organizations such as Friends groups and trustees, vendors, literacy groups, and all types of libraries and library organizations.

ABOUT THE AUTHORS

BECKY CALZADA is the district library coordinator of the Leander (TX) Independent School District. She is also a cofounding member of Texas #FReadom Fighters and is the president-elect of the AASL for 2024–25. She was selected for ALA's fourth Policy Corps cohort, works as a member of the Policy Corps' cadre for Proactive Advocacy on Book Banning, and is a member of ALA's Intellectual Freedom Committee. Becky is the recipient of several intellectual freedom awards and was honored by *People* magazine in their 2023 Women Changing the World portfolio.

VAL EDWARDS is the library team leader in the Madison (WI) Metropolitan School District. She has experience working in a variety of library settings. Val has trained as a conflict mediator and published articles in both library/education and business publications. She has served on several ALA/AASL/Core committees, was the AASL division councilor, was a past chair of the Core Library Consulting Interest Group, and currently serves on the AASL's Bylaws & Organization Committee.

MAEGAN COFFIN HEINDEL is the library services coordinator for the Madison (WI) Metropolitan School District. Her background includes both school librarianship and classroom teaching. She is an alum of ALA's Emerging Leaders program and served as the AASL's Learning4Life coordinator for Wisconsin. A frequent conference presenter, Maegan has held multiple positions in the Wisconsin Educational Media and Technology Association and the CCBC's Friends Board. Maegan is currently a member of the CCBC's Charlotte Zolotow Award Committee.

INDEX

A

action plan
    designing and launching, 33–40
    outline of, 41–43
administrators
    core documents and, 66
    information gathering and, 65
affinity exercise, 64
allies, internal, 13
American Association of School Librarians (AASL), xi, 48
American Library Association (ALA), 3, 14, 61, 65
assets-based lens, 15
Association for Library Service to Children (ALSC), 18

B

board members, information gathering and, 65
board policies, 11–12
"broken record" issues, 31
"buddies" model, 58

C

capacity-building, 57–62
challenge readiness
    initializing plan for, 1–24
    inside-out diagram of, xvi*fig*
    introduction to, xv–xvii
    operationalizing plan for, 25–53
    systematizing plan for, 55–77
challenges
    balancing demands of, 44–46
    case example of, 48–51
    current context for, 3–7
    increase in rates of, 3, 4*fig*
    initial response to, 42
    from outside community, 42–43
    role of pre-planning for, 5–6

Chrastka, John, 73
city council meetings, 12
clarity, 36
coaching for conversations, 59–61
cohesive action, readiness for, 27–32
collaborative priority-setting, 10
communications
    addressing concerns and, 27–28
    as advocacy, 68
    consistent, 58–59
    creating pathway for, 35–36, 35*fig*
    emotions and, 48
    expectations regarding, 59
    impact of actions on, 59*t*, 60*t*
    information gathering and, 18
    plan/planning for, 33, 63–70
    sample language for, 28
    scheduling conversations, 36
    scripting language, 46
Communications Department, 67
community culture and climate, 11, 12
community support, 43
concerns, addressing, 28
conflict, 31, 47–48
consistency, 36, 58–59
conversations
    navigating as coach, 59–61
    scheduling, 36
Cooperative Children's Book Center (CCBC), 4, 5*fig*, 13
core documents, 66–67
culture and climate
    community, 11, 12
    notes on, 15–16
    workplace, 9, 14
curricular materials, 21, 71
customer service, 44

D

definitions, xvi
diplomacy, 44–45
discussion groups, 30–31
district leaders, information gathering and, 63–64

E

emotional reactions
    awareness of, 48
    reducing, 45–46
    responding to, 44–45

F

FAQ documents, 67, 68
forms for reconsideration, 21–22

G

governing board, 66

H

Hart Research Associates, 61
Huggins, Melanie, 74

I

I Am Jazz (Jennings), 73–74
inclusion, cultivating, 29
infographics, 67
information delivery, 68
information gathering, 17–18, 63–66
inquiries, addressing initial, 42. *See also* challenges
institutional priorities, 12
intellectual freedom, stated support for, 20
interlibrary connections, 13
internal allies, 13

INDEX

J
Jennings, Jazz, 73–74

L
language, care in using, 46–47. *See also* communications
Legal Department, 67
Lenski, Tammy, 43
Library Bill of Rights, 4, 20
library displays, 22
Library Journal, 73
library programs, 22
local organizations, like-minded, 13–14

M
management-level leaders, information gathering and, 63–64
media attention, 72–73
meeting protocols, 10
models, national, 13

N
National Coalition Against Censorship, 65
national models, 13
national partners, 14
newspapers, as resource, 12
North Star Opinion Research, 61

O
Office for Intellectual Freedom (OIF), 3, 4*fig*, 14, 18, 20
onboarding, 38, 38*t*, 57–58. *See also* training
organization chart, 45*fig*
organizational guidelines, 11–12
organizations, like-minded local, 13–14

P
parameters, statewide, 12–13
patron-centered mindset, 11, 44
PEN America, 4, 14, 65
playbill perspective, 31
policies and procedures
　access to, 66
　considerations for, 20–22
　current, 11–12
　distinguishing between, 19–20
　elements of, 18–19
　evaluating, 17–18, 20–23
　importance of, 22
　notes on, 23
　review team for, 18
positive relationships, building, 11
preparatory training, 30–31
preparedness planning, xv–xvii
pre-planning, 5–7
priorities, institutional, 12
priority-setting, collaborative, 10
process improvement tools, 64
psychological safety, 28–29
public library board meetings, 12
public-facing documents, 67–68

R
readiness, ongoing, 57–62
reading associations, 14
reconsideration policies
　access to material and, 20–21
　committee makeup and, 22
　current, 11–12
　elements of, 18–19
　evaluating, 17–18
　familiarity with, 72
　on multiple requests, 22
　toolkit for, 18
rehearsals, 46, 60–61
research, sharing, 61
resolution mindset, 41–53
resources
　for community culture and climate, 12
　supporting, 13–14
　team as, 14–15
response capacity, 29–30
response guidelines, 45–46, 45*fig*
response team
　action plan for, 36–38
　identifying, 34
rollout framework, 36, 37*t*

S
scenarios
　applying plan to, 71–76
　facilitating discussions of, 46–52
school board meetings, 12
scripting language, 46
"Selection & Reconsideration Policy Toolkit," 18
selection policies
　elements of, 18–19
　evaluating, 17–18
　familiarity with, 72
　reviewing, 11–12
　toolkit for, 18
self-assessment, 9
self-censorship, 3
Sinek, Simon, 68
social media, 43–44
solo librarians, 39
space, providing, 29
staff training, 27, 38, 38*t*, 41–53, 57–58. *See also* onboarding
stakeholders
　communication plan for, 66–68
　needs of, 63–66
state partners, 14
statewide parameters, 12–13
support staff, core documents and, 67
survey data, as resource, 12

T
team
　information gathering and, 17–18, 65
　ongoing needs of, 57–58
　psychological safety for, 28–29
　as resource, 14–15
　scenario discussions and, 46–52
　See also response team
team preparedness approach, 72, 73, 74
Texas #FReadom Fighters, 65
"Toolkit for Program Challenges," 1
toolkits, 18, 65
training, 27, 30–31, 38*t*, 41–53, 57–58
train-the-trainer model, 58
trust, 29

U
unified approach, 14
Unite Against Book Bans, 65

V
values
    identifying, 11
    transparency regarding, 31

W
workplace culture and climate, 9, 14

www.ingramcontent.com/pod-product-compliance
Lightning Source LLC
Chambersburg PA
CBHW082044250426
43661CB00080B/2785